Praise for

READ MY HIPS

"Kim's voice is refreshing, real, brutally honest, and laugh-out-loud funny. Her words paint a vivid picture that is completely relatable. In my work or in my life, I have never met a woman (of any age, size, or shape) who did not experience body image issues or some degree of self-loathing. Kim poses great thought-provoking questions and her message is uplifting . . . Love yourself as you are—no matter what your size and shape—you are already *whole!* A fabulous, fun read! Thanks, Kim, for your bravery."

—Laurie Sliva, founder, director, and life-skills trainer, B.R.I.D.G.E.S. Programs for Girls

"In *Read My Hips,* Kim entertainingly advocates a revolutionary way of being: accepting our here-and-now bodies as we are and with love. With wit, sensuality, and realistic logic, she shares her journey through time and transformation, baring her attitudes and discovering antidotes for our society's limited and limiting way of seeing our bodies. Kim's sensuous love of the world and all its prickly details makes for a delightful and moving read."

—Debora Iyall

read my hips

How I Learned

to Love My Body,

Ditch Dieting,

and Live Large

read my

KIM BRITTINGHAM

hips

THREE RIVERS PRESS
NEW YORK

Copyright © 2011 by Kimberly Brittingham

Published in the United States by Three Rivers Press, an imprint of
the Crown Publishing Group, a division of Random House, Inc., New
York.
www.crownpublishing.com

Three Rivers Press and the Tugboat design are registered trademarks
of Random House, Inc.

Library of Congress Cataloging-in-Publication Data

Brittingham, Kim.
Read my hips : how I learned to love my body, ditch dieting, and live
large / Kim Brittingham. — 1st ed.
p. cm.
1. Brittingham, Kim.   2. Overweight women — United States —
Biography.   3. Body image in women — United States — Case
studies.   4. Self-esteem in women — United States — Case studies.
5. Women — United States — Psychology — Case studies.
6. Reducing diets — United States — Case studies.   I. Title.
RC628.B69 2011
362.196'3980092 — dc22
[B]   2010042801
ISBN 978-0-307-46438-5
eISBN 978-0-307-46439-2

Printed in the United States of America

BOOK DESIGN BY ELINA D. NUDELMAN
COVER DESIGN BY JESSIE SAYWARD BRIGHT
COVER PHOTOGRAPHY © STIEF & SCHNARE/SUPERSTOCK

10 9 8 7 6 5 4 3 2 1

First Edition

FOR AUNT PHYLLIS AND PERONNE

CONTENTS

PART THREE: LIVING LARGE

The stories in this book are true. In many instances I really do recall, almost verbatim, dialogue from as far back as three decades ago. But in other instances, I've done my best to re-create dialogue that feels accurate in both word choice and sentiment. In the case of phone messages from executives of 5W Public Relations, I still have word-for-word transcriptions of the messages as left on my answering machine. I jotted them down thinking I might use them in a blog entry; I wound up using them in this book instead. A few scant details of these stories have been changed as the years have simply erased various specifics from my mind—and some on purpose, in order to protect the privacy of others. I have also changed most names, including that of the weight loss center where I worked, in the interest of privacy.

When I was a teenager, my mother took a picture of me standing in front of our house.

I stood unsmiling beside a flowering bush. I knew I was bigger and uglier than most girls, but maybe the camera would strike a deceptive angle and make me look pretty.

When the picture came back from the developer, I was mortified.

I was going to make sure no one *ever* saw this awful image of me. I stole it from its paper envelope and scurried away to my room.

I sat on the edge of the bed and stared at the semigloss print in my hands. I had no idea I was so misshapen! I knew I was pear-shaped; all the women in our family were. But genetics had hung themselves on my frame with an unnecessary flourish of cruelty. My hips ballooned out from my body, in freakish contrast to my trim waist. I was an extreme, like those apes with shockingly bulbous red bottoms.

I began to cry. *My God,* I thought. *I'm deformed!*

Clearly, I'd have to cover this up. Never again would I wear a shirt or sweater under thirty-two inches long—or at least not until I fixed this problem. I'd wear tunics and dumpy cardigans, and men's button-down shirts three sizes too big, just because they covered my hips.

I took the photo to my desk and with a fine-tipped black marker, oh-so-carefully, I shaved several inches off my hips, applying the ink in parentheses-like strokes until I'd blacked out the swells of excess flesh. I sat up straight and regarded the image of myself with a "normal" body, and felt overcome by a surge of shimmering hope.

Pure possibility. It coursed through my veins like warm, flowery bathwater. The promise of improvement, of being better than this flabby, self-conscious, blemished sack of flesh I dragged between home and school every day. The suggestion that I might actually *become* the heroine of my daydreams. It was irresistible.

I could make it happen.

I'd just go on a diet.

I don't ever remember my mother being fat, and yet I clearly remember her dieting. When I was growing up, she read many women's magazines — *Redbook, Family Circle, Woman's Day.* As a stay-at-home mom, she watched daytime talk shows like *Donahue.* She was immersed in the popular culture of the day and so, like millions of other American women, she was exposed to the media onslaught of "thinner is better" messaging, both overt and covert.

There was this glossy two-page spread of diet tips by Richard Simmons that she'd cut from one of her magazines and taped to her bedroom door. One of his suggestions was to use tiny children's utensils for eating, because it would help one ingest less food. Above the type was a photo of a hammy Richard in a red polo shirt with white collar, holding a goofy oversized knife and fork, one in each hand, his mouth and eyes agape in comic exaggeration.

We moved around the country a lot, every couple of years or so. And everywhere we went, my mother carefully folded and stowed away her Richard Simmons diet tips, only to unfold and retape them to the bedroom door at our new address. The old tape grew brittle beneath the new, deepening to an unhealthy-looking, jaundice color and flaking away.

My mother started her diets — and eventually, our shared family diets — very gung ho. There were inaugural trips to the supermarket, during which she stocked up on foods we usually *never* saw in our house. Like cottage cheese. She made lots of sweeping "from now on" statements: "We won't be eating this *anymore*." "We're going to start taking walks *every night* after dinner." "Things are going to change around here!" She made charts for each member of the family on which we could track our exercise, and in the case of my brother and sister and me, our chores and our homework, too (because sweeping dietary change was usually concurrent with recommitments to pitching in around the house and getting straight A's). At the stationery store, Mom bought multicolored, star-shaped metallic stickers we could lick-and-stick to mark our daily victories. She experimented with her blender and we swallowed things made from powders. She made me get up an hour early and go jogging with my father before school. Jogging made me feel like I couldn't breathe, and I hated being forced into *his* company. The mood inside my Mork and Mindy lunchbox was dismal. Snack cakes and aluminum peel-top cans of pudding were gone. Sandwiches became wretchedly thin. We were eating special bread now — diet bread, from the pink bag, sliced super-thin, "...so you can have *two* slices for the same number of calories as a single slice of regular bread!" my mother enthused. "It saves a whole bread exchange on Weight Watchers."

Fortunately, the upheavals never lasted more than a week.

I'm not sure if my mother tired of all the extra effort it took to prepare these "diet" meals, or if she tired of the bland foods themselves, or of my ceaseless complaining because I'd been coerced into doing leg lifts with her on her bedroom floor. I just know that seven days later, the mashed potatoes and meatloaf would be back on the menu, the Ring Dings would return to the pantry, and no one talked about the cottage cheese going rancid in the back of the fridge. We were relieved. We knew Mom would get inspired again, eventually, but until that happened, we were keeping our traps shut.

It was only a few short years, though, before I'd become a teenager, and then I'd be the one initiating the diets, requesting them, asking for *Jane Fonda's Workout* album for Christmas; and doing leg lifts by myself, on my own bedroom floor. I didn't want to be fat anymore. I wanted to fit in. I wanted to be immune to the kind of disapproval I read in the eyes of every thin person who ever looked at me.

I can't blame my mother for imbuing me with the "diet mentality," because we coexisted in the same ugly culture. There was already something wicked at work that was far bigger than either one of us—a rapidly burgeoning, manipulative, and self-serving diet industry working from behind a mask of false benevolence.

Throughout my teens and adulthood, I enjoyed many moments of triumph on the scale—at home, at the weight loss center, on the big pay-scale in the drugstore. But there were just as many moments of frustration, desperation, and deprivation as I undid all the dieting I'd done. Dieting was the express train to "let's see just how fat this girl can get." It sped me through all the "weigh" stations along the route, rarely stopping to rest long at any one victorious weight loss. In between, it delivered heartbreaking telegrams via scale that revealed ever-increasing all-time highs. I started at 145 and dieted my way down to a gaunt 128. I reveled in those 128 pounds for five minutes before the weight began to creep back up, and just two months later I found myself at 155. The pattern continued, down and up ever higher, until one day, I peaked at 310.

Multiple go-rounds with Weight Watchers, Nutrisystem, and daily home deliveries of "Zone" diet meals made those companies richer. Sure, they brag they can "fix" you, but they never tell you up front about that one percent success rate. And when you fail, it's never their fault. *You've* got something wrong with *you*.

I used to beat myself up for being such a failure, a repeat failure, unable to control myself. But in recent years I've read about what dieting does to our minds and bodies, and there's evidence that once we start consciously tinkering with our food intake in an effort to reduce our body size, our bodies pull out every weapon in their arsenals to prevent us from succeeding. It seems no amount of "willpower" can overcome the body's need to protect us from external threats to the food intake we're used to. Reducing our caloric intake can actually trigger a narrowing of focus in our *minds,* too, a survival mechanism that makes sure we obsess about food until we get enough of it. Unfortunately, the whole act of self-deprivation — even mild self-deprivation — is so unnatural that we respond by eating more than we really needed in the first place.

All those years of trying to lose weight exacerbated my

already-unhealthy relationship with food. I was an emotional eater from a young age. Dieting casts an even bigger spotlight on food and all the accompanying rigidity; all those "forbidden" foods only made me want them more.

Once upon a time, food was fuel for my body and a pleasure to my senses. But it became so much more. Now it's supercharged with meaning and burdened with responsibilities it never signed up for.

Besides, the widely swallowed message that no pursuit is holier, more righteous or valiant, than the pursuit of lost pounds fostered unnecessary self-hatred in me that took years to undo. Every weight loss program, no matter how positively it's packaged, whispers to you that you're not right. You're not good enough. You're unacceptable and you need to be fixed.

I officially reject that message. I reject it for myself, and I reject it on your behalf, too.

I wish I could go back in time and convince the adolescent girl I was to accept herself *just the way she was*. I'd tell her she was "ready" already, and she'd know what that meant. I'd tell her that every second she spent thinking about weight loss was shaving a minute off her life. I'd warn her that the bigger the deal she made out of eating less, the more she'd *want* to eat. I'd beg her, from the floor if necessary, to cry more — cry as hard as her bellyache was deep.

I wrote this book because I can't consult with my younger self. The best I can do is tell my own story, and hope that anyone currently romping with the devil of body hatred, scale-watching, fat phobia, or dieting will finally wake up from that wasteful nightmare and live in authentic bliss.

You're about to take an intimate peek into my experience as a female living in America in the 1970s through the present, and how the cultural obsession with thinness in my time and place helped shape both my mind and my body. These stories aren't presented linearly — we're going to jump around in time a bit. But I've organized them in three sections, around three themes about which I feel passionate: "Ditching Dieting," "Loving My Body," and "Living Large." You're going to recognize much that's familiar in my stories. Sometimes you might even feel like I'm writing *your* life. Don't be surprised. If you're alive with me in my times and have grown up in the Western world, we probably have startlingly similar thoughts and experiences around food, weight, and body image — even if you're drastically thinner or fatter than me. Even if you've suffered from an eating disorder that I haven't. Even if you think your self-image and eating habits are relatively healthy.

What if you woke up tomorrow morning to discover that your body, the way it is now, is considered the ideal body? What would you do if you never had to worry about the size or appearance of your body again?

Maybe like me, you'll laugh more. And I hope you'll wear exactly what you want to wear, whether it's polka-dot 1950s party dresses, pin-striped suits, or overalls with pink high-top sneakers. I hope you'll feel like the best character in the best movie you've ever seen. I hope every day, you'll find a new fascination. I hope you'll make somebody else's day, every day. I hope you'll sing loudly with the windows down while driving. I hope you'll feel a little smarter each day, and be OK with what you didn't know yesterday.

Today, I can look in the mirror and, regardless of the shape, size, weight, or texture of my body, I can see myself exactly as I really am and *still* feel motivated to build a life of greatness around that body. I don't feel like there's a crucial piece missing — that piece being "thinness."

I've also vowed never to consciously try losing weight ever again. And make no mistake, there's no unhealthy complacency in this approach. I will continue making efforts to eat more healthfully. I'll continue to explore foods of good nutritional quality. I'll continue to address with curiosity the reasons I eat in the absence of physical hunger. I'll try to respect my body while strengthening it.

I accept my body and try to be as healthy and happy as possible *while fat*. Hey, maybe some of my healthy habits will result in weight loss *anyway,* but that'll just be another naturally occurring change like any other. Like muscles forming in response to a repeated activity. Like graying hairs. Like beginning to menstruate, or stopping. I will not be watching the scale.

In 2008 I appeared on the *Today* show, and beforehand the producer requested that I provide pictures of myself at different stages in my life. As I was digging through a box of old photos, I came upon the picture of myself with the inked-out hips.

Obviously I couldn't see the true shape of my body beneath the black marks, but I paused and studied my fifteen-year-old cheekbones, chin, torso, and upper arms. *Hm, that's strange. I thought this was my Fat Picture.*

I carried the photo to my kitchen table, hovered with a damp cloth, and finally rubbed away the crescents of black ink that recontoured my hips. It came off easily; the picture was like new.

I couldn't believe what I saw.

Underneath the ink, there was almost . . . nothing.

But . . . but I *remembered* this picture! I remembered
hunching over it alone in my bedroom, making delicate cor-
rective strokes on an *embarrassingly disproportionate girl*.

What happened to the hips? Those big goiterlike hips I
fantasized about cutting off with our electric Thanksgiv-
ing turkey knife? Where were they? I *remembered* seeing
them there! I know I did, I looked *ridiculous*! They were so
awful, I'd been willing to do *anything* to get rid of them. I
was determined to diet those hips off my body before I got
stuck with them for *life*!

There was nothing wrong with the girl in the picture.

God, how I wish someone could have told her.

PART ONE

DITCHING DIETING

When we lose twenty pounds…we may be losing the twenty best pounds we have!

We may be losing the pounds that contain our genius, our humanity, our love and honesty.

—*Woody Allen*

RING DINGS

I'd dreaded this day. Dread like a belly bruised from the inside, swirling puke green, putrid purple, and horrid yellow, and dripping black droplets like lead. At five years old, I wasn't sure I knew how to pray, but the night before in the quiet of my mind, I'd given it a whirl and pleaded with God, "Please don't let us move to Michigan tomorrow. Please." Maybe God was more powerful when you were sleeping under a picture of Jesus, I mused. Jesus tacked to the wallpaper with a neat red pushpin. Jesus in a white tunic with outstretched arms seated on a rock, beckoning to children and snowy lambs drawn with shy, humanlike smiles. Maybe he was most potent when you prayed to him from the bed of your religious grandmother, and prayed with an aching heart.

The night before was our final night in Philadelphia. With our furniture already loaded onto a big green-and-white Bekins truck and motoring toward Detroit, we spent the night at my grandmother's. I insisted on sleeping with her. I snuggled against her back and was serenaded softly by the radio playing "church music," as she called it — a spiritless choir delivering correct and measured hymns. Its blandness soothed me.

When my mother roused me in the morning, Grand-mom was already up and I found myself alone in her bed, wrapped in the worn-soft cotton sheets dotted with tiny blue flowers. It was five o'clock, that eerie time of day when the world seemed painted in watercolor and sound was shrill, as though delivered through a too-loud television. A teaspoon clattered on a metal stove top, a rustling bag chafed my ear. The air smelled of wet tree bark and coffee.

"Come on, sleepyhead."

I was in no mood to cooperate. I didn't want to con-tribute to anything that would hasten my separation from Grandmom. I adored that chubby, sweet-smelling lady more than anyone in the universe. What I wanted was to stay right here with her, forever, in this ugly rented sand-colored bungalow on Solly Avenue.

She appeared in the doorway behind my mother.

"You better get up, there, kiddo," she scolded gently, and reluctantly I sat up. As much as I objected to our im-minent departure, and would've been willing to handcuff myself to the radiator had I the resources, I still couldn't bring myself to disobey Grandmom. The thought that I might cause her grief in any way shattered me.

I was sitting on the edge of the bed, propped up like a rag doll, groggy and limp, when my mother told me to lift my arms. She pulled my cheap, staticky nightgown over my head, the tag that ensured its inflammability scratch-ing up my side. She slid a turtleneck back over my head. I squinted at myself in the dresser mirror. My grandmother came and settled at my side and smiled at me in the glass, then reached out to pat my knee. I leaned irresistibly into her and she curled an arm around me.

"Sit up straight so you can put your pants on," my mother commanded.

"I don't want to go to Michigan!" I cried. "I want to stay here with Grandmom."

"If you want to come back and see Grandmom again at Christmas, you'll be a big girl and stop making such a fuss."

Why not leave me here with Grandmom, and you can come back and visit us both? I wept, my face bunched stiffly up and glowing a bitter pink, my lashes heavy with clinging tears. I wanted to beg her, *Please, Mommy. I can go to the school around the corner, where the playground is.*

My little heart throbbed inside my chest and my stomach heaved, as though my organs were squeezing out tears of their own in there. My chin tensed and my bottom lip trembled as I buried my face in my grandmother's belly.

"Grandmom, oh Grandmom . . . !" I clung to her.

I could hear my mother sighing impatiently behind me.

"Kim," she said. I heard my own breath catch in my thickened throat. "Kim!" she repeated, angrier this time. I turned my head, still pressed into my grandmother, and saw my mother from the corner of my eye, holding two small brown buckled shoes in her hands.

My grandmother's hand patted my head gently. "You've got to get your shoes on, kiddo," she urged.

Daddy came to the door and wondered out loud, "What's the situation?"

I hated the way he said that. Sit-chew-WAY-shin. He always wanted to know what the sit-chew-WAY-shin was, always with his big paws set belligerently on his hips.

"Well, are we gettin' on the road here or what?"

I didn't like the way things changed after my mother married Daddy. I didn't see Grandmom as often, and my mother quickly learned that the most efficient way to bribe me was with currency of grandmother: "But I'll take you to see *Grandmom* on Saturday..." It was the magic word. I'd do anything she asked.

I didn't like living with a big mustached dad who came walking in the front door right in the middle of *The Jeffersons* with his shirt all torn up, stinking of "aftershave" and his knuckles dripping blood. I didn't like the way Mommy leapt from the sofa and ran to him to nurse his taproom wounds. In my humble kindergartner's opinion, she was never nearly angry enough for the sit-chew-WAY-shin. If it was me, I would tell him to get lost.

I especially didn't like it when Mommy brought my baby brother home from the hospital, and my parents beamed over him like he was the neatest thing since the disposal cigarette lighter. She held the squirming bundle out to me, so I could have a look.

Oh, how I wished she would take him back, but I knew darn well that Mommy couldn't return the baby the same way she'd return a box of weevil-tainted Rice-A-Roni to the corner store. Still, I asked, "Is he staying forever?"

My mother let out a dry laugh. "Of course he's staying forever. He's your brother. He's a part of the family."

I, for one, didn't want to be a member of this family. Something about it just felt...I don't know. So *phony*. It was like I'd been enrolled in playing half-hearted house with a bunch of kids I'd never really liked that much. I wanted to grit my teeth and snarl under the towering shadow of my father, "You don't belong to me, you big *bully,* you," then turn to the baby in his stupid foofy blue bassinet and point a finger into his screwed-up little pink face, "...and *you* don't belong to me either, you poopy-smelly baby," and then spin around to face my mother and shout, "and *you* don't belong to me anymore because *now* you belong to *them*!"

But I didn't say anything. I was just a little kid, and nearly everything was out of my hands.

I surrendered and stepped into my Buster Browns and let my mother buckle them, all the while keeping one of my small hands tucked inside my grandmother's. I considered dropping to the floor and begging to stay, but I could imagine my mother's biting admonishment, *Oh for Christ's sake, do you always have to be so dramatic?* Maybe she really wouldn't bring me back to see Grandmom at Christmas. Maybe she meant that. Just in case, I kept my mouth shut.

That day we drove for ten hours to a rectangular three-bedroom house on a tree-lined street with cracked sidewalks, with roots breaking through from below. I cried nonstop for the first two hours on the road. That vast and terrible feeling returned to my heart every time I pictured my grandmother's sweet, smiling eyes tinged with a watery sadness of their own, and my belly turned over and moaned. The sockets of my eyes seemed pumped with poison, the backs of my eyeballs were burning. Weirdly, I detected the fleeting alcoholic whiff of a doctor's office. I squeezed out a hot spring of tears.

I whispered, "I miss you, Grandmom."

I let my head hang forward. When I opened my eyes again, a long glassy ribbon of snot was hanging from the tip of my nose, dangling perilously over my lap. I brought my shirt up to my face and blew. As I pulled it down again, wetter now and heavier like a dirty rag, Daddy thumped his fist against the steering wheel and shouted at my mother, "Jesus, this kid's been crying since we left Philly! Enough is enough already. Can't you find some way to shut her the hell up?!"

My mother leaned forward and reached into a paper

grocery bag snug between her feet. She burrowed her hands inside, then drew them out again. She held something white. She swiveled around in her seat and offered it to me.

"Here," she said. I reached forward and took the little package into my hands. It crinkled.

"Ring Dings," the label read.

I tore open the plastic and that distinctive aroma of chemical chocolate met my virgin nostrils. I reached in and pulled out a little brown cake, like a sticky hockey puck. I bit into it and a surprise creamy-sweet white center seemed to smile on me. The cake filled my mouth, then slid into my belly, padding it. It packed itself like a plaster against my seeping wounds. I ingested more cake; my stomach grew fuller and was soothed.

I consumed my very first Ring Ding. The ache subsided. My tears dried, I grew quiet. I thought of Grandmom again after I finished the cake, but only briefly. For there, in the bottom of the package, was a second one.

GLORY DAVIS MADE ME BELIEVE
IN TOTAL TRANSFORMATION

Samantha: Hey, but a lot can happen in a year. You could come back next fall as a completely normal person.

Farmer Ted (considering for a moment):...Really?

Samantha (shrugging): Sure.

—Molly Ringwald and Anthony Michael Hall in *Sixteen Candles*

Some people are guided through life by the model of Jesus Christ. They even wear bracelets reminding them to inquire, What Would Jesus Do? But my adolescent self was guided by the image of a fantasy me: the hypercharged, ultimate version of myself I believed I was destined to become when I grew up. I was thirteen years old when I first started pruning and polishing my vision of her. She was like a religious icon, screen-printed on a Santería bodega candle glowing steadfast, deep within my doughy teenage middle.

My fantasy self was beautiful, because beauty inspired admiration. Ugliness didn't cut it. Ugliness never won. And since there was no such thing as being beautiful without also being thin, my fantasy self was necessarily slender. She had unnaturally elongated legs, but with just the right amount of muscle tone. She strode around Manhattan in miniskirts and heels, taking wide, purposeful strides, flashing toothy grins over her shoulder at her obvious admirers and hailing taxis with energetic flair. She was a walking tampon commercial, or a fast-paced ad for shampoo. At any second she might wipe at her eye in close-up, then show the clean pink pad of her index finger, demonstrating that her mascara wouldn't smudge.

My fantasy self had the kind of confidence I didn't have — confidence enough to take charge of her dreams and make them real. And assisting her in the achievement of these dreams would be the entire world, hypnotized by her feminine charms, refusing her nothing. Everyone would willingly rush to her aid. The world would fall in love with her. The world would always say yes. They'd find nothing about her unacceptable.

In my teen daydreams, I liked to project ten or fifteen years into the future. I figured it gave me plenty of time to transform from frumpy teenager into fluffy-haired heroine. I was always a witness in these daydreams, as though watching my future summed up in one big-budget, epic music video. Sometimes I saw myself through the eyes of an adoring stalker. Other times I pictured myself from the point of view of some specific person, and tried to imagine how they felt about the "me" they were observing. Sometimes the witness was a celebrity crush, sometimes a non-celebrity crush. Other times, it was my mother, and she always felt proud of me.

For a long time I didn't think about how or when the transition would happen. Almost smugly I enjoyed the carte blanche of being a kid. Penniless, jobless, with a room of my own and a lock on the inside door. I was someone to whom Santa still paid visits; I could still be claimed as a dependent. I had time yet to be fat and ugly with crooked, gappy teeth, unmanageable hair, and social anxiety. Being a teenage misfit is far more bearable when one is confident that her adulthood will be notable, magical. I had time yet to dream of a better future. I had the luxury of trusting that the planets would eventually align and morph me into my superfine self, in plenty of time to spend my entire adult life enjoying it.

It wasn't until the first day of school in the eighth grade that I felt the true ferocity of my own desire to change. That day, I was struck by a fever of possibility—smacked by the reality that total transformation can, in fact, occur; that talk show–variety makeovers really did happen to kids my age, in small, inert Tennessee towns without Chinese restaurants, where no one knew what a bagel was. I realized I could be the proactive sculptor of my life, sooner rather than later. It was an irresistibly promising and powerful thought. Glory Davis lit the flame.

Glory Davis and I went to junior high school together. In seventh grade, we were not yet friends—still mere acquaintances, although we had things in common. We were both chunky girls, fairly quiet on the whole but less restrained among our friends; polite to our teachers but never as sugary sweet as they assumed us to be; always standing just outside the sphere of what was considered fashionable and peering in.

In seventh grade, Glory Davis wore oversized men's turtlenecks and discount-store jeans that were snug around her ample derriere but wide and baggy in the legs—long after the look was first fashionable, and at least twenty years before its return to vogue. Her thick chestnut hair was parted simply in the middle and hung exactly as it grew: long, straight, and weighty, cascading over her shoulders and obscuring her burgeoning bust. She had a double chin as her yearbook photo attests, and a little belly that, like mine, formed a roll over the waistband of her jeans when she sat.

Meanwhile, I was doing my best to dress like a London New Waver in little suede ankle boots that had a tendency to collapse above the heel and outdated men's clothes I found at the back of my dad's closet. You wouldn't have discerned much about my shape by looking at me, and that was the idea. I was thick in too many places. I had to buy *ladies* jeans to accommodate my round butt and the little mound of my stomach. Dad's black-and-red houndstooth overcoat was gigantic on me, but it made the specifics of my figure impossible to see. Besides, I fancied it looked like the oversized jacket David Byrne from Talking Heads sometimes wore. I rolled up the coat cuffs and clustered glossy pinback buttons on the lapels. I felt I'd struck a perfect pitch halfway between hiding my temporary imperfections and claiming my particular place in the pop culture continuum.

Glory Davis departed the seventh grade with a homely wardrobe and a chubby butt, legs, and belly. But after three quiet months, she returned to Vance Junior High School and strutted a new and improved product into the eighth grade.

Wow. *Glory Davis*. Her summer transformation was *the* thing to talk about. The cadence of her name scampered up and down the corridors. It was uttered discreetly from behind shiny new Trapper Keepers. It was whispered from one head to another behind open locker doors, and warbled up from the bottoms of ceramic urinals sounding curdled and profane. Glory's metamorphosis from one grade to the next seemed miraculous.

Glory would no longer be considered chubby. She was

svelte and curvaceous, with a plump but compact rear end and a generous thirteen-year-old bosom, enhanced by a tidy nipped waist. She'd had her hair cut into a style of the day that flattered her, with glossy waves at the back of her head and soft feathers framing her face. She'd always had a touch of caramel latte in her skin, and over the summer she'd tanned deeply and evenly. It made the green leap from her eyes. The baby fat around her face melted away and revealed gentle, pretty features, a softly pointed chin, showstopping dimples. She'd always had strong-looking, straight white teeth, but now she didn't hesitate to show them.

Glory and I became friends that year, when we landed in the same art class and appreciated each other for refusing to make jokes about flatulence or feces. We considered them base and unsophisticated. "Hillbilly humor," she used to call it.

Glory Davis never looked back. She didn't revert to her seventh-grade self for any half-baked reason, not even in an emergency. Her mind had been sanitized of all firsthand knowledge of frumpery. She knew nothing of striking a downtrodden pose — how was it done? Her eyes never betrayed a moment of self-doubt. Her backbone seemed incapable of collapse.

Those dumpy clothes must have been set afire. But the new Glory didn't dress with the desperation of total imitation, either, a fact for which I still have immense respect. Glory had no desire to play a pathetic, wanna-be second fiddle to Bitty Parker, our would-be prom queen and ringleader of the popular girls.

Glory stood apart. She was discriminating about the trends she adopted. Yes, she wore shapely designer jeans, but instead of a prudish polo, she paired them with wildly ruffled pseudo-Victorian shirts with puffed sleeves (tucked *in,* and not a belly roll in sight) and matching low-heeled pumps. She looked more like a guest star on *Hart to Hart* than some country club fruit salad. She was better than this place.

And Glory was kind to everyone. She didn't turn up her nose at the shoeless kids with dirt-smudged faces that the school district brought down from the mountains and forced to go to school. She didn't withhold her smile from a snorting flock of prep queens, even if their greeting was insincere and only to be followed by a hushed insult and a group cackle as Glory passed.

And somehow, over the course of just one summer, Glory had learned how to flirt. I don't know who taught her how to giggle and swat at our art teacher Mr. Logan without causing a major incident. The new Glory was a skillful schmoozer, and I mean that in the most complimentary way. She made small talk sound like honey and mercy, delivered center stage from beneath a spotlight. She endeared herself to administrators and parents alike, even my own mother, who took to Glory instantly.

And the boys—well, they absolutely adored Glory. They bumbled after her like hounds. Unadoptable shelter hounds with ever-so-slight brain damage and drooling problems.

Boys didn't look at *me* once, let alone twice. Me, the walking overcoat.

Glory Davis was the very first person to demonstrate to me that radical personal refashioning really could happen, and the way she sported that change made me want it for myself. I wanted that kind of complete turnaround that gave people whiplash: "Oh my God . . . Kim, is that *you?*" How could *I* do what Glory had done? Glory, who at our junior high graduation ceremony, made everyone gasp in unison. Even parents. She made the in-crowd look positively dowdy that day in their uniform of madras plaid, calf-length skirts, penny loafers, and oxford shirts; the girls from the "right" housing developments, the Melissas, the Kristins, and Pams. Glory flashed a toothpaste-commercial smile and kept her gaze on a point just an inch or two above the horizon, then sashayed down the center aisle of folding chairs on our gymnasium floor, wearing a fire engine red dress with fluttering sleeves and a skirt made of six tiers of georgette. A simple pendant rested against her tan décolleté. She was the only girl in our class who could have worn that dress so well, and she knew it, and the world forgave her for it.

One night that autumn, I lay on my twin bed, on my stomach, up on my elbows, with a clean notebook page before me and a blue ballpoint pen in one hand. I began taking a thorough inventory of my flaws, literally from head to toe. Hair, eyebrows, skin, nose, ears, lips, teeth, arms, belly, hips, hands, thighs, heels. I scribbled a long list of everything that needed to be perfected physically, then added *wardrobe* and *personality* at the bottom.

Then, to the side of each physical feature on the list, I made a smaller checklist of steps I could take to improve it. I tore other pages from the notebook and created daily and weekly schedules incorporating these steps—*hundreds* of steps—working them into time slots before and after school, and after dinner. It was a rigid, full, and unforgiving regimen.

I was developing a personal boot camp on my way to total transformation.

When I was in the thick of boot camp, revved up with fervid determination, I exercised every day of the week for at least two hours. It wasn't fun, but my will to be thin sustained me. I did twists at the waist and leg lifts. I jogged in place. I planned a week in advance every crumb I'd put into my mouth. Foods I loathed. Carrot sticks. Yogurt, which smelled of vomit. I was determined to lose as much weight as quickly as possible. So fast, people would positively marvel at me.

I brushed my hair every evening, one hundred strokes on each side and two hundred strokes in back, to stimulate natural oils and combat my tendency toward frizz. I applied a growth formula to my eyelashes before bed. I rubbed a skin-lightening cream into my finger joints, because they were a shade darker than the rest of my hands and I thought they looked funny. I steamed my pores wide open and cleansed my face raw. I exfoliated my heels, whether I needed to or not. I practiced sculpting my nose to appear more narrow, using different shades of brown and beige eye shadow.

I rearranged my closet and drawers and made an exhaustive record of every possible combination of separates. Every night I wrote down what I would wear the next day, right down to the earrings, and tacked it to the back of my bedroom door. I checked books out of the library on etiquette and the art of conversation, and I copied the information by hand into spiral notebooks, as a way to better assimilate the data.

I was afraid of dentists, but I had a gap between my two front teeth wide enough to fit a third tooth, and I was self-conscious about it. I felt as long as I had this gap, my chances of being pretty were nil. So I fashioned homemade braces out of a paper clip, curling two hooked ends of a crooked length of metal around my teeth to urge them together. I wore them in the privacy of my bedroom for as long as I could stand the pressure.

And oh, how I felt the passion! I wanted to show myself

and the world that I was a winner. A gal who had it all together, worthy of singing the Enjoli perfume jingle:

> *I can bring home the bacon!*
> *Fry it up in a pan!*
> *And Never, Never, Never let you forget You're a man!*
> *'Cause I'm a Woman!...Enjoli!*

I also drew before-and-after pictures of myself, as a
motivator. I drew the "after" me thinner — much thinner
than I could ever humanly be. I drew myself as a sticklike
figure without curves of any kind. Like a Popsicle stick
with a head, dressed in Vivienne Westwood leather. And
I wasn't a child with limited artistic ability, either. You'd
realize this immediately if you'd seen the "before" picture.
But somehow, I knew what a proper "after" picture should
look like, and it more closely resembled the classic stick
person than realism. Smaller was virtuous. Smaller was
pretty. Smaller was everything a girl should want to be.
A better body was one lacking in all bumps and bulges,
whittled clean of protrusions and humps.

I recognized the difference between the "before" and
"after" pictures of dieters in my mother's women's magazines. Before and after pictures were plastered on the walls
of her Weight Watchers meeting place. Richard Simmons
was always going on television with his most successful
disciples, and their "before" photos were usually projected
onto the back wall of a talk show set — "morbidly obese"
people with hands folded on top of giant bellies. But then
the "after" would come strolling out from backstage,
holding his or her former fat jeans between two wide
outstretched hands, and the audience would roar with approval. The host predictably laughed, "You can fit your
whole body into *one leg* of your old jeans now!" Make-

overs got great ratings. New hair, the right rouge, a blouse from the appropriate Color Me Beautiful palette ("Louise here is a summer, but her entire life she was wearing autumn colors that made her look sallow"), tied up in a bow the happy shade of twenty pounds lighter. I saw it everywhere. It could be done. People could change themselves entirely.

I didn't hang my before-and-after drawing out in the open. I kept it tucked in the back of my Snoopy wallet, next to the group picture of Duran Duran and a *TV Guide* clipping of a youthful Timothy Hutton. I didn't want other people knowing what my plans were. I cringed at the thought of anyone else realizing my secret wish to be thin and pretty. If they knew, they might crush my dream, tell me before I even tried that I would never, ever win. They might convince me that no matter what I wore or weighed, I would never be good enough for widespread acceptance. I was unwilling to hear it.

I was determined to summon all my strength, all that remarkable raw human *will* that made desperate mothers lift cars to free their pinned offspring, that made soldiers turn back and dart through the crossfire to save a baby-faced, fallen Oklahoman in fatigues. I was feverish with possibility. *Yes,* I vowed. *I'll tap that power!* I had a noble goal and I would achieve it. I would become so smart, charming, disciplined, and wise, that I would maintain perfection in every area of my life.

Before drifting off to sleep, I thought very hard about the fantasy me, thinking so hard that my eye sockets felt sore. I made up mantras and whispered them over and over again, in case some godlike entity was listening and might come to my aid. *Be the perfect me. Make the dream real. Transformation happens.*

Inevitably, though, my rigid boot camp lifestyle started

breaking down. I couldn't sustain it. I started eating things outside of my plan, succumbing to intense cravings for all the foods I wasn't allowed to have, like Ring Dings, peanut-butter-and-jelly sandwiches, and those crispy shoestring potato sticks that came in the peel-top can. One good wheezing attack and I was scared away from exercise. I was bitterly disappointed in myself for failing.

Glory and I were standing in the lunch line in the school cafeteria. I'd brought my "diet lunch" from home, having relocated my will of steel and recommitted to boot camp, but I always bought my skim milk at school. I looked over Glory's shoulder, at the pink melamine tray she held in her hands. A rectangular, cardboardlike slice of institutional pizza lay at its center, and its upper corners were balanced by a paper cup of grapes and a carton of milk, respectively. She turned to me and glanced at my tiny milk carton in one hand and the brown bag I clutched in the other.

"You bring your lunch on Pizza Friday, too?" she questioned.

"I didn't used to," I sighed. "But I've been trying to lose weight and I'm not doing so great. I brought half a turkey-and-mustard sandwich. Glory, tell me something. What did you do to get so skinny? And how are you not getting fat again eating like that?" I nodded in the direction of her pizza.

She gave me a strange, blank look, then slowly turned her gaze on the pizza.

"I don't know," she shrugged. And just like that, it seemed the conversation was over. But I didn't want it to be. No. I was standing there, waiting for answers. In fact, when we eventually got to our table, I intended to whip out a pen and paper and take notes.

I prompted her again. "No, I mean, what did you eat over the summer? Every day?"

We approached the cashier and Glory put down her tray and began digging into her change purse. As she placed the silvery coins into the lunch lady's raw, waiting hand, she gave me a quick glance, her eyebrows furrowed in confusion and her mouth kinked up on one side.

"Every day?" she repeated. "Kimberly Anne, how in the world do you expect me to remember *that*?"

"In general," I corrected, quickly handing the lunch lady my dime and scurrying after her. "I just need to know what worked for you," I lowered my voice as we approached the matrix of lunch tables crowded with jawing eighth graders.

When we were finally tucked in neatly at our own table, with our lunches laid out before us, Glory shrugged and shook her head. "I didn't do nothin'."

And that really was the end of the conversation.

She doesn't want to share the secret, I thought. *She wants it all to herself.* I was disappointed, but not bitter.

For a long time, the fact that Glory Davis hadn't purposely gone on a diet or attended charm school that summer was completely lost on me. I don't think she engineered her own transformation as tooth-gnashingly as I tried to engineer mine.

Maybe all that happened was that someone told her she was beautiful, and maybe for once she believed it.

BACON-CHEDDAR MELT

It's called ketosis, and the secret came my way through a nutritionist named Dr. Penza. He gave free consultations in a health food store called Dudley's, from inside a storage closet concealed by a batik curtain.

I'd waited my whole young life to stumble upon an enchanted formula like this. Finally, the one thing that really *worked*. Finally, I'd be set free from the burden, the handicap, the universal suit of rejection that was fatness. From here on out, life was going to be paradise. I'd be unstoppable.

I loved going to Dudley's. I felt healthier just being there. It *smelled* like good health, like burlap sacks of just-harvested grains—and metallic minerals that smelled vaguely of blood. Nice clean blood, though, blood that ran bright with vitamins. There were shelves of unsalted, corn syrup–free breakfast cereals and organic soups, freezers full of free-range meats and tofu burgers, a Peg-Board hung heavy with packets of raw herbs, condiments from country kitchens and foreign lands. Whenever I emerged from Dudley's biting into a big, hulking bar of organic chocolate, I felt like an Olympian-in-training.

Dudley's was exotic, too. The walls were adorned with

Dudley's personal mask collection: African masks, Mexican masks for La Dia dos Muertos. Dudley and his wife were old hippies. He looked like Jerry Garcia from the Grateful Dead, with a big, bushy gray beard, and he always wore a pith helmet. Mrs. Dudley was satisfyingly spooky with long, frizzy black hair streaked with silver. They weren't chatty folk. They shared the same mysterious, quiet countenance. You just had to trust that in their silence, they were wishing you vibrant health and wellness. Like a prayer.

My friend April and I went behind the curtain to see Dr. Penza together, like two girls on a double date insisting on going to the bathroom as a pair. He was sitting at a small round table surrounded by lawn chairs and cases of couscous. He was a long, thin man with a trim gray beard, and he stated everything as though it should already be obvious.

"So what do you girls want help with today?"

We sank into two aluminum-framed chairs with orange canvas seats.

"Do you have any advice for us on how to lose weight?" April asked.

Of course it's what she asked. She didn't ask about premenstrual syndrome or cancer prevention, or fertility, or how to eliminate leg cramps, headaches, or flatulence. Between us, April and I talked about weight loss incessantly. We talked about getting thinner, always in the context of it being good for our health, but really we just wanted to be more attractive. We waxed nostalgic about how lanky we'd been in kindergarten, evidence that we weren't *meant* to be *this* fat. Therefore, pursuing thinness was not only the right thing to do, it was returning us to our true nature. We reminisced about the near-ideal weights we'd once been, however briefly. We showed each other items

of clothing we'd kept for years in the back of a closet, saying, "Can you believe I actually *wore* this tiny thing?" and
vowed with a determined edge to be able to wear it again.

"Maybe there's an herb that can stimulate the metabolism?" April prompted the doctor. I never thought about
herbs before I met April. I saw her as a wise, holistic sort
of person. She wanted to do things the natural way, and
that made sense to me.

"Well, if you want to stimulate your metabolism, bladderwrack's always a good bet." Dr. Penza shrugged. "But
if you want to lose weight, losing weight's easy. I don't
know why the world makes such a big deal out of it. Just
put your body into a state of ketosis. You'll drop weight
like that." He snapped his fingers.

We both leaned forward an inch or two. He had our
complete attention.

"What's ketosis?" I asked predictably.

"Look." Dr. Penza leaned back in his chair. "All you've
got to do is cut carbohydrates out of your diet. Eat all the
protein you want, all the meat, all the cheese, all the milk.
And leafy green vegetables, those are okay too. Your body
burns carbs for energy and turns the excess carbs into fat.
So if you don't give it anything new to burn, your body
will turn on itself and start burning its *own* fat for energy.
The weight'll melt right off you."

"But aren't milk and cheese fattening?" I asked.

He let out a short laugh. "Oh, that's the beauty part. You
don't have to worry about fat. Don't even *worry* about it;
doesn't matter. Fat in foods is good for your body. Your
body needs it, makes your skin and hair shiny." He gestured limply toward his own deeply lined face and thin-
ning head of hair. "If you don't believe me, try it out for a
week. Then you'll see."

April had taken a scrap of paper out of her purse and

was scribbling down notes. "So it doesn't have to be low-fat cheese? Or skim milk?"

Dr. Penza shook his head. "Nope. I'm telling you. Eat all the protein you want, no carbs. Get up in the morning, have some bacon, a nice big steak, make yourself a Swiss cheese omelet. You'll see. And if you want, a couple drops of bladderwrack tincture under the tongue, but that's not even necessary."

I couldn't believe that could really work. Bacon, cheese, steak? All you can eat, and lose weight?

"Something about this doesn't seem healthy to me," I said, having already decided I was doing it anyway.

Dr. Penza let out a heavy sigh and his narrow shoulders rose and fell sharply. "The fact is, you could eat total crap all day, every day and be fine. Any of us could. If you're in a good place spiritually and emotionally, it doesn't matter what you eat. Maintaining a state of complete serenity is like wearing a suit of armor against disease. The problem is, you don't know how to manage stress. Most people don't. So instead, you have to watch your nutrition."

April covered her scrap with notes. "Okay, so, leafy green veggies are fine, right?"

"Sure, sure. Lettuce, spinach, eat all you want. You know, I was an architect for many years," said Dr. Penza, "but I decided I didn't want to die young like everyone else in my family. Right now I'm the only one left. All of my brothers and sisters, my cousins, they all dropped dead in their forties. I became a nutritionist so I could keep myself alive. And I have." He reached into his shirt pocket. "Here's my card," he said, handing it to April. I couldn't wait to get out of there. I wanted to get started on some pork chops smothered in cheddar and test this guy's theory.

April and I quickly discovered that the world runs on carbohydrates.

In the beginning, avoiding carbs was fairly painless. For breakfast, I ate yogurt. Plain yogurt. Rich, creamy full-fat yogurt, but I added artificial sweetener and a drop of chocolate extract to keep things exciting.

I took my lunch to work. I layered turkey lunchmeat and sliced pepper jack cheese, then rolled them up together and pierced them with toothpicks. Like protein cigars. Completely breadless. I was working in a temporary secretarial assignment then, side-by-side with polite strangers. I wonder if they ever talked about me after I left that gig, remembering "the weird temp who ate all her food in cylinders."

Eating in restaurants was a challenge. No matter what the cuisine, April and I wound up with the same thing: plates laden with pathetic puddles of sandwich ingredients, untidy and fatigued looking, lying down in surrender when stripped of their buns, breads, or tortillas. Every dining experience was a downer.

For dinner at home, I ate beef patties, but I couldn't eat them plain—that was too dreary. I needed a topping. Ketchup wouldn't do, because it was loaded with sugar and sugar was a carb. Instead, I discovered a brand of ketchup at Dudley's that was made in the Amish country, sweetened with apple juice. Yeah, apple juice was technically still a carb, but I figured it was making less of an impact on my weight loss efforts than regular ketchup. I slathered my breadless burgers in melted cheese and all-natural ketchup and ate them with... well, with relish. Every bite was bringing me closer to a new me, radically transformed.

And the weight melted off my body. Just like Dr. Penza said it would.

"How can this possibly be *working*?" April marveled. "Isn't all this fat bad for us? God, we can eat all the eggs and bacon we want!"

After a couple of weeks, the sight or smell of meat, cheese, or eggs made me want to puke. Everything I put in my mouth seemed thick and oily.

But I persevered, encouraged by the speed with which my body was changing right before my eyes.

"Gargoyle Lady lent me a bunch of clothes." I spoke of my landlady, a sixty-something woman with an unfortunate habit of contorting her face in unflattering ways when she spoke. I rented the back bedroom of her modest Philadelphia row house.

"Lent you clothes?" April repeated. "You mean, her own?"

I nodded. "Yeah. She said my clothes were practically falling off of me. I guess she took pity on me, because she invited me into her room and started taking all these suits out of her closet, saying I could wear them. I don't know, it felt weird. It's not like I know her that well. But she was so excited, I agreed to try one on."

April broke in. "What size?"

"Eight. And it *fit*." I grinned and we gave each other a high-five.

I was at work. Another one of those temp jobs in a downtown high-rise where I got paid to do nothing for hours on end. Although at this particular assignment, now and then, they coughed up something for me to do—like working miracles with their filing cabinet.

"All these files need to be put away," the guy told me, pointing to a tower of overstuffed files slumping into a corner and climbing against the wall like manila ivy. I didn't have a problem doing that kind of grunt work—the problem was, there was absolutely no room left in the filing cabinets. I shoved as many of the files into the drawers as possible, moved files forward from one drawer to the next to spread things out. But eventually, there was nowhere else to go.

"Kim, why are there *still* files stacked in that back hallway?" asked the balding consultant with an overinflated sense of his own importance.

"The file cabinets are full," I replied. "Remember? I told you that two weeks ago. I have no place to put them."

He looked rapidly from his left to his right, as if the solution was a lieutenant waiting in the wings to be commanded.

"But—but that can't be, there's gotta be someplace to put them...." And he stalked back to take a look for himself. Another two weeks later, I'd hear from him again. "Kim, I thought I told you to put away all those files in the back hallway?" It was moronic.

During one of many quiet hours, I was sitting at my desk under the soothing whoosh from the air-conditioning vent and fantasizing about french fries, hot fudge sundaes, and buttered toast. Saliva cascaded through my mouth and flooded the gulleys beneath my tongue. It was a step beyond imagining I could taste them. I was *sensing* them. I *was* a hot, crisp, salty french fry.

Years later I would find myself at a nightclub with a flavored oxygen bar, where I allowed a bartender in a professionally pressed golf shirt to thrust a clinical-looking plastic piece up my nose, which delivered mango oxygen from a long rubber tube and deep into my sinuses. I could neither taste nor smell mango, but my brain was registering MANGO in an eerily complete way—as though I'd merged with the fruit.

It wasn't entirely dissimilar to what I used to feel when I was on a diet, and I'd daydream about some forbidden food. I felt myself dissipating on a cellular level and becoming one with the food. The tiny molecules that, somewhere on the planet, were gathering to form a slice of whole wheat toast were zooming through space and time to meld with me.

One morning as I kept my desk chair warm, alternating between dreaming of bread and brainstorming ways to solve the world's crises, I felt an unfamiliar sensation in my chest.

It felt like there was a fist wedged just beneath my breastbone, and suddenly, it clenched itself. Hard.

It frightened me.

I put my flattened palm against my chest and rubbed the area. I inhaled deeply, made sure I could still breathe. I glanced around me in panic. I wanted to ask somebody, "Did you see that?" I took my fist and thudded against my chest, to restart my heart in case it had stopped. I checked my pulse to make sure the thing was still beating. I smiled at one of the younger consultants passing by, hoping he'd say something to me, just one word, because if he acknowledged me, then I must still be here—I wasn't dead.

I didn't have my own doctor. I didn't have medical insurance. But I had volunteered for a paid medical study not long ago. For two months I took an anti-anxiety medication, or a placebo. I'll never know which. And I was taken in a taxi once a week to a doctor's office where a medical student ran through a list of anxiety symptoms and asked me to rate the intensity at which I'd felt them during the previous week. Every three visits, a beefy physician with a kind face and tightly curled brown hair took my blood pressure, my pulse, samples of blood and urine. I remembered his name, so I called him.

"There's nothing wrong with you, everything seems normal," he said, removing the stethoscope from his ears.

"But how can that be?" I asked, shifting my ever-decreasing weight on the examination table and hearing the crinkle of clean tissue beneath me. "Did I tell you about the diet I'm on? It must be all that meat and dairy fat clogging up my arteries. My heart can't take it."

"You have the cholesterol of an Asian," he said. "All the Chinese and Korean people I see, who eat all that rice and fish? You've got cholesterol comparable to theirs. I think what you felt was a muscle spasm."

Crap. How could I prove him wrong? I thought about all the methods he probably had at his disposal for really, truly confirming that my heart was thick with plaque and failing. I suppose he could stick me on a conveyor belt and send me through one of those claustrophobic machines that scans your body. I'd seen one in a TV commercial and thought, *God, having to lie inside one of those things for an hour would be* worse *than dying.* I wonder if they have a panic button inside that'll shoot you out the open end in a mental emergency, or if it's entirely under the technician's control? Well, that would just be *hell.* Scratching that possibility off the list, I reasoned that the only other way to really confirm all that deadly fatty buildup was to open me up surgically—and I wasn't keen on that option, either. Besides, who would pay for it?

I could only hope that I'd die in my sleep. In a deep sleep, so I wouldn't have to endure those torturous moments of *knowing* I was going to die.

"If it happens again, put a hot compress on your chest. It'll relax the muscles."

"But you don't understand," I said. "This felt like it was coming from deep, deep within the center of my chest. Not on the surface."

"Like a heart attack?" He shook his head. "You're too young for a heart attack."

But I wasn't convinced. Surely someone, somewhere in time, had died of a heart attack at the age of twenty-three.

There was a second squeeze, and it seemed to last two seconds longer than the first one. It happened in Gargoyle Lady's kitchen, just as I was sitting down to a meal of burger patties smothered in pepper jack cheese.

I pushed my chair back from the table and gasped, giving my breastbone a little thump. I was breathing heavily in alarm. I picked up my plate and made my way to the garbage can, where I dumped the food right into the bag and waited to stop shaking.

It occurred to me that there might be another way to deal with this congestive heart failure thing. Maybe if I gave up the ketosis stuff, my arteries would clear themselves out. Maybe I was still young enough to bounce back like that. Maybe if I ate lots of clean, fat-free carbohydrates and drank gallons of water, I could flush it all out. I imagined long, translucent strands of spaghetti bloated with water, like tapeworms the color of angels' wings, snaking through the pipes of my heart and dragging out clumps of snotlike cholesterol with them.

Spaghetti, I thought. *We need to get some spaghetti right now.*

After all, I'd lost all that weight a couple of years earlier eating big bowls of ziti with fat-free creamy Italian dressing, and cornflakes, and pretzels. I decided I'd rather find a slightly slower way to lose the weight, and live to see myself reach my goal.

April persisted on her ketosis diet. Hers was a bit different from mine, though. Even more limiting. She had an intolerance for many things, or so she believed. "I can't eat eggplant because I'm allergic to the pigment that makes

the skins so dark. I know from experience. Even if I re-
move the skin, there are still traces of it in the vegetable.
And I can't eat anything that begins with a 'p,' because I
read that it counteracts with my pitta-kapha nature. I also
read in a holistic health magazine that oregano contains
an enzyme that gives you mouth sores, so I have to avoid
anything that might have oregano in it and take caplets
of L-carnitine to get rid of my cold sores. Oh, and I also
know, through trial and error, that anything with wheat,
cocoa, tomato, or citrus gives me insomnia."

On one hand, I wanted to respect what April thought
she knew about herself. But on the other hand, I sometimes got the feeling she was just full of it. Not on purpose;
I don't think she realized it herself.

"Um . . . this gazpacho—does it contain eggplant?"

The waitresses always started out so pleasant and patient. "No, no eggplant. It's mixed vegetables but I know
eggplant isn't one of them."

"Well, what kind of broth is it?"

"It's like a tomato-based broth . . ."

"Oh! Oh no. Nonononono. Can't do that. I guess I have
no choice but to read this menu again, huh?" April sniffed.
Her eyes scanned the menu and she sighed. "Is this turkey
sandwich served on bread made with wheat?"

The waitress looked confused by the question.

"I mean," April continued, "do you have any kind of
bread that's gluten-free?"

I started to feel embarrassed for being with this pain-
in-the-ass woman. I really, really didn't want the waitress spitting in our food. I wanted to tug on her apron
and whisper, "Just remember which one of us ordered the
penne à la vodka. It was the one of us who was agreeable
and easy to please."

"I . . . don't know, I guess I could ask the chef . . ."

"Oh never mind!" April barked, annoyed. "How 'bout this Tuscan chicken, does it have any oregano in it?"

The waitress nodded slowly. "Yeah. I'm pretty sure it does."

April huffed and looked at me as if to say, *What's the matter with these fucking restaurants? Haven't they learned yet how to create tasty dishes from hot water and lawn trimmings? I mean, get with it!*

"I guess I'll just have a salad then," she said, slamming her menu shut. "But no dressing. Just bring it to me plain. Thanks."

And then, at that little round café table with its fresh white tablecloth, overlooking a window box full of artificial daisies, I was struck by the total absurdity of it all. Until I'd given up on the ketosis diet, this is what I must've looked like, too. Frustrated. Out of my mind. Angry that there was something wrong with me because somehow, the rest of the world could eat whatever it wanted and not get as fat as me. This wasn't how I wanted to feel every day of my life. It was almost like being someone with a rare medical condition who had to weave her life around dozens of behavioral restrictions and never quite felt normal. Almost like forcing oneself to live like a diabetic to avoid getting diabetes, without ever knowing if you'd have gotten it anyway.

I was pretty sure April's insomnia and herpes had nothing to do with tomatoes, oregano, or anything else edible. Her lifestyle of extreme limitations was self-imposed. She was unhappy with her work as a cleaning lady. She was unable to control the behavior of her simpleton boyfriend and his two rambunctious kids. But here was something she *could* control. My circumstances were different, but from deep within, I felt a pang of recognition. I understood that need for control. The need to be the master over food

and feel like a strong, commanding woman. If it seemed
I was failing in life by earning too little money, in jobs
that held no meaning for me, here was something that offered the illusion of progress. I felt like a loser because everyone else my age seemed to possess inviting sitcom-like
apartments with comfortable furnishings and cute cars,
and they jetted off to Cancún for long weekends without
a second thought. Meanwhile, for me, advancement was
ending the month with enough money in one lump sum to
pay for a discount bus pass. But on any given day, I could
feel like the most powerful being on earth by maintaining
flawless, rigid control over what I put in my mouth. On
any day when I adhered perfectly to my diet, I went to bed
feeling invincible, enlightened, and buoyed by spiritual
muscle.

Just days after abandoning ketosis, the weight started
creeping back onto my body. It made itself at home on the
backs of my hips, clinging like two baby koalas. It hugged
my middle like the arms of children encircling me, one
child over another over another, piling into a silly, giggling
group hug. I dragged them along with me as I walked.
They were heavy. I was out of my landlady's borrowed
clothes within a week and I gave them back, draping them
neatly on the iron banister just outside her bedroom door.
My belly and hips were soon marred by blood red zebra
stripes, a quarter of an inch wide in spots. I didn't know
what they were until I showed a friend who had children.
"Ah, stretch marks," she nodded in recognition. "I got
them in my third trimester with Daniel Jr." That was how
quickly the weight came back on. I was terrified to resume
ketosis. I'd been scared straight. And I'd met someone
at work who told me ketosis was bad for you. It ruined
your kidneys, she said, "and once those go, you're dead."
I didn't know what to believe, but I was personally con-

vinced that my heart had taken a hit. Besides, human beings had been eating bread for thousands of years. It didn't
seem logical that we should do without.

I looked to food for comfort from my fear of getting
fat again, fear of being unable to make the rent, fear of
keeling over from the damage I'd already done to my
body on all that meat and cheese. I missed carbs so much,
I ate more than I needed or even wanted. I boiled huge
pots of pasta, stocked the freezer with half gallons of ice
cream—the cheap stuff, from a regional dairy—and I ate
and ate and ate.

Eventually April announced she couldn't go on with this
ketosis thing.

"I can't do this shit anymore," she proclaimed, unload-
ing a package of pita bread from her grocery bag.

"Yum. We haven't had this in a long time," I smiled,
taking the bread bag lovingly into my hands.

She sat across from me and pulled her chair close under
the table. "Yeah, I got it at Dudley's. Mmmm, wow, this *is*
good. Oh! And something else."

She reached back into the brown paper bag.

"Look what else they had. This tea. Look, it says it can
help you lose ten pounds in seven days. And it's all natural. A lady in the store saw me with the box in my hand
and said she tried it. She said she lost a *ton* of weight the
first week, but it gave her explosive diarrhea and stomach
cramps. I think I can live with that, though, as long as it
works."

I put down the bread and took the pink box into my
hands, brought it close to my face, greedily ingested its
promises.

"We can share if you want. I think that's a two-week supply."

I opened the box and took a deep sniff. Cinnamon. I pulled a tea bag out of the box.

"No reason to wait. Want a cup?"

WE WERE THE WEIGHT LOSS COUNSELORS

I walked into the stockroom of the Edie JeJeune Weight Loss Center to find a flock of white-coated weight loss counselors shoving chocolate-covered peanut butter bars into their mouths. They were standing among half-open cardboard shipping cartons, their well-manicured hands clenched around crinkly torn wrappers.

Renay looked up as I entered, then moved forward to drape her arm around my shoulders. "Hey, everybody! Have you all met Kim? She's new here. She doesn't know about the shelf of damaged goods yet."

Katie, DeeDee, and Julia all turned to look, their jaws chewing away.

Renay reached into a nearby carton and removed a gleaming new box of Edie's Eaties peanut butter bars, then dropped it forcefully to the ground. "Oops!" she said with comic exaggeration, then plunged the heel of her pink pump into the heart of it, and twisted. "Tsk tsk. These shippers really should be more careful. Looks like we have more damaged merchandise here, ladies!" They cackled like ravenous witches. Renay tore the top off the box. They descended upon her.

I don't know how Edie JeJeune operates these days, but when I worked for them in the early 1990s, Edie JeJeune Weight Loss Centers sold their own prepackaged food as part of their diet plan. They called the food Edie's Eaties. Part of our duties as "weight loss counselors," as we were called back then, was to unpack the shipments when they arrived at our center and put the food items on shelves and into freezers, where they'd eventually be picked and bagged by the receptionist for our dieting clients. Every now and then an item arrived from the warehouse that was damaged in some way — usually a crushed box corner or a dented can of tuna salad. Damaged packages had a designated shelf, where employees could take whatever imperfect merchandise they wanted, free of charge.

At all times, there was an open "damaged" box of peanut butter bars for the staff's at-will snacking. It was positively uncanny how boxes of peanut butter bars got mangled, mutilated, punctured, and crushed on their way from the Edie JeJeune warehouses more frequently than any other food item.

The Edie JeJeune peanut butter bars really didn't taste that great. The chocolate coating was thin and waxy, and the peanut butter insides had the dense consistency of sawdust and glue. But they had a mysteriously addictive quality. I've since learned that foods with just the right ratio of sugar, salt, and fat can be almost as addictive as cocaine, so maybe that was part of their allure.

I went to work as an Edie JeJeune weight loss counselor because I thought it would get me, and keep me, thin. It seemed a foolproof plan — total immersion in a "thin" lifestyle. How could I not become a thinner, healthier person in such an environment? I reasoned it would work on me the way working as a picture framer once put such great framed art on my walls. I would fully incorporate into my life what was in my awareness every working day. I'd take it home with me.

As soon as I signed on as an Edie employee, I went on the Edie JeJeune weight loss program. I got Edie's Eaties at a discount. All new counselors were encouraged to go on the Edie plan from the beginning, so we'd know firsthand what we were talking about when we discussed it with our clients.

Even so, I would've gone on the program anyway. I'd gained weight since my last diet, but I was going to try again, and try harder. I didn't intend to be the kind of person who just lies down and gives up. I wanted more for myself than that.

My primary job as a weight loss counselor was to keep clients buying Edie's Eaties from week to week. All Edie JeJeune clients received preplanned weekly menus that incorporated Edie's Eaties from breakfast through dessert. Brand-new clients would browse the menu and sometimes say, "Oh, wait—I see there's tuna salad for lunch three out of seven days this week. I don't like tuna."

As counselors, we were trained to respond to this sort of thing by saying, "We encourage all new clients to stick with the menu as-is for the first two weeks—no substitutions. This will give you a chance to try all the Edie's Eaties we offer. Then if you have any objections, we can consider substituting the tuna day with a different menu day altogether."

"But I really don't like tuna," the client might insist. "I don't need to try it. I *know* I'm not going to like it."

Our next response was supposed to go like this: "[Insert client's name here], I'm here to do everything I can to make sure you succeed on the Edie JeJeune program. That's why we want you to stick with the menu as written for the first few weeks, so you'll have a chance to try all the foods. Variety is an important tool in keeping you motivated to stick with the program."

Our manager suggested not showing new clients their first week's menu *before* they left the center. Instead, she instructed us to have their Edie's Eaties prepacked into bags when they came to the front desk to pay and to simply slip the bag handles over the client's hands as she was departing — *before* she could too closely examine the bags' contents and see what foods she was stuck with. This way, she wouldn't have a chance to object. Edie JeJeune didn't like having to deal with food substitutions unless it was absolutely necessary.

I really didn't want to push tuna salad on someone who hated the stuff. In fact, I couldn't think of a better way to encourage *cheating* on the diet. Briefly I thought, *Of course, if someone cheats, they'll lose weight more slowly, possibly even gain some weight. That would mean they'd have to stay with Edie JeJeune even longer, and buy even more weeks of Edie's Eaties.* I dismissed the thought and scolded myself for being so cynical.

In the beginning, I was a good Edie JeJeune employee. I performed all my required duties. I looked over each client's food diary, gently inquired about any deviations from the prescribed menu, then entered his or her food order for the week. But the part of the job I genuinely enjoyed was connecting with people. The weight loss counselors had their own assigned clients with whom they met on a weekly basis. I loved my clients. And my clients loved me. Sometimes they brought me little gifts; they knitted me things. They told me things like, "You should be a motivational speaker!" and "Coming here and talking to you makes me feel like I can do *anything*!" I really did believe my clients could do anything, and I told them so. I didn't always limit conversation to their weight loss goals. I was interested in their lives. I believed they *could* go back to school at night, start that business, get that promotion. They just had to find a way to tap in to their personal power.

Melissa was the manager of the center where I worked. She was a short, pear-shaped woman in her midtwenties with dark hair and freckles. Melissa found it difficult to speak without shouting and she blinked rapidly when challenged in any way. She didn't look at all like the women from Edie JeJeune "corporate," regional and district managers who visited periodically to peer over the manager's shoulder, run meetings and trainings, and intimidate our eager-to-please receptionist. Women from corporate weren't always severe, but they *were* always beauty-pageant pretty and flawlessly polished, from their patent leather pumps to the white tips of their French-manicured fingernails.

We weight loss counselors attended continuing education sessions about once a month—workshops on topics that were intended to help us, and our clients, succeed. They were called CEs.

"What can we do when a client is struggling?" Nancy, our regional trainer, asked one evening during a CE. Nancy was a poised, six-foot-tall Vanna White look-alike.

An eager counselor named Viki raised her hand, and Nancy pointed at her with a Magic Marker.

"We could remind them of what motivated them to come to Edie in the first place?"

"Goooood!" Nancy drawled. But when she said it, it sounded more like "guhhhh ee-yud!"

Rose-Marie spoke without being called on. "We could try to find out what's wrong with them. I mean, like if they're depressed or something."

Nancy tipped her head to the side like a shih tzu detecting a high-pitched whistle. "Well, you're half right. We do want to find out what's going on, and what obstacles are keeping the clients from sticking to the program. But we're not psychologists, so it's not their depression we want to address. Our job is to keep the clients on the *program*."

Nancy approached an easel at the front of the room that held an oversized pad of paper. She flipped up the pad's cover to reveal a clean page and wrote the word *Tools,* then underlined it with a flourish.

"I know some of you like your clients very much and want to help them through their personal troubles. And that's very suh-weeeeeet." Nancy heard that whistle again. "But one of the kindest things we can do for our clients is to get them using *all* the Edie tools available to them."

Her eyes scanned the sea of white coats before her. "How many of you can honestly say that all of your clients are using the Edie JeJeune walking tape?"

No one raised a hand.

"I have one or two who use them," Rose-Marie piped up.

"How many of you can say that all of your clients, and I mean *all* of them, are using the Edie JeJeune *motivational* tapes?"

Again, no hands.

"Well, there you go! Clients who use the Edie tapes are much more successful than those who don't. The tapes are an opportunity for you to jump-start your clients' success. And don't forget, you get a *ten-percent commission* on every set of tapes you sell. That's ten percent of the price, directly into *your* pocket." She smiled and a tiny point of white light winked off an incisor.

The Edie walking tape was a singular cassette with rousing, Sousa-like music and voiceovers by Edie JeJeune herself, meant to be listened to while walking for exercise. The motivational tapes came in a huge set—about a dozen different cassettes—in a big spongy case with little cassette-shaped spaces in a plastic liner where the tapes could be nestled for storage. The tapes included recorded messages from Edie JeJeune on different topics meant to educate and keep the client focused on results. The walking tape was reasonable in price, but I remember the motivational set being shockingly expensive. I listened to them once, just to familiarize myself with the content, and found Edie's advice too obvious to really be helpful.

One night a week, weight loss counselors were required to stay late. We were forced to call people who'd dropped off the program and try to convince them to restart. It was excruciating. These people didn't want to hear from us. Melissa dug deep into the file cabinets and withdrew aging files going all soft and fuzzy at the once-sharp manila corners. Then she dropped them onto our desks, two dozen at a time.

"Whoever gets the most return clients scheduled on their books will win a hundred dollars," she announced one evening. "The only catches are these: the client has to have been inactive for at least three weeks, and they only count if they *show up* for the appointment. Merely *scheduling* the appointment isn't enough."

"But Melissa, some of these people say they just can't afford to buy the Edie's Eaties," I argued. "How am I supposed to counter that?"

"Tell them that you're still their counselor, and that you're here to help them with their weight loss goals, no matter what. Just tell them to get in here and talk to you, that's all."

If I was lucky enough to actually get one of these drop-outs on the horn, they were usually exasperated and irate. They were tired of being nagged by us, they said. But now that I had Melissa's green light to invite them into the center to simply be counseled, I found that getting them to return was fairly easy.

"Look, I'm here to help you. Don't waste me as a resource," I told them. "Just come in one night this week. We'll talk. You don't have to buy any Edie JeJeune food. Just come in and talk to me and we'll figure out a way to get you back on track."

I won the hundred dollars. My book was jam-packed for the next two weeks.

One day in a staff meeting, Melissa announced that our center had developed a low revenue-per-client average.

"I've looked at our books, and we have plenty of people coming in," she said, "but this means they're not *spending* what they should. All of your clients should be purchasing full weeks of food, unless they're on maintenance or going on vacation. What's going on? Are you selling people partial weeks of food?"

Everyone was looking around at one another and shrugging. But I understood what was happening, immediately.

"Melissa," I said, "we have all those people who dropped out and then rescheduled during the contest. A lot of those people can't afford to buy the food, remember?"

She frowned and dropped her arms stiffly to her sides, as if in disbelief. "Are you saying none of those people have restarted buying the Edie's Eaties yet?!"

"Well, no!" I replied. "You said to tell them to come back into the center, just to talk."

She laughed like I should have known better. "Well, yeah, but you can't keep them coming and taking advan-

tage of counseling without buying the *food*!" She guf-
fawed. "I mean, we won't make any money *that* way!"

"But wait a minute..." I sat up a little higher in my
chair, annoyed.

"It's fine to *lure* them back that way, Kim. But the goal
is to get them back on the food within a couple of weeks."

But these people can't afford *this overpriced dog food,* I
thought, gritting my teeth. I swear to god, I wanted to
walk right up to the front of the room and pound my fist
into her jaw.

I understood what it was to want to be thinner, but I
was seeing something at Edie JeJeune that was driving
people insane. Most of my clients dropped out before
reaching their goal weight. Some had been on the program
forever, yo-yoing up and down the scale within the same
fifteen-pound range. Of the hundreds of people I weighed
and counseled, only one woman made it to her goal weight
and went on the "maintenance" program.

Sometimes my clients were teary and apologetic for failing, as if they expected to disappoint me. More often, they
were angry with themselves, seething like some short-
tempered barroom bully, a coiled spring just waiting to
release and knock off somebody's block. They snarled at
themselves, "I'm such a loser!" They demanded to know,
"What the hell's the matter with me?" Clients who'd had
less experience with anger wept bitterly instead, confess-
ing from their thickened throats, "I hate myself."

Other times they might slump into the chair beside my
desk like an apathetic teenager whose parents were making her go to Edie JeJeune. I'd try to draw answers out
of these clients. What was going on? What was keeping
her from sticking to the menu? These clients weren't forthcoming. They shrugged a lot. I wasn't sure how to address
them. After all, it was their choice to come to Edie, yet

they were giving me the semisilent treatment, as though I was a familiar and despised torturer. As though they'd developed a strategy for surviving the hell I was putting them through by shutting up and taking whatever food, menus, or advice they were given, regardless of whether they'd actually use any of it.

"Same time next week?"

"Yep," came the spiritless reply, and they'd depart with their bag of Edie's Eaties, most of which would go uneaten in favor of something tastier.

Some clients kept coming in from week to week and eating the Edie's Eaties, *in addition to* other food from the real world. As long as they kept coming to the center and shoving Edie's Eaties down their throats, they retained a sense of hope. As if they believed that failing to show up at Edie JeJeune would curse them to fatness forever. As if the Edie's Eaties had some magical quality of canceling out the fat and calories of any non-Edie food that was consumed the same day.

Meanwhile, I felt more in control of myself than I ever had before. Life was looking good. I had my Edie's Eaties, and I knew how to use them. For the first time in my life, I felt a very definite sense of relief at not having to think so hard about what and when to eat. That burden had been lifted. All I had to do was look to my Edie menu and eat what I was told. *Life* should *be this way,* I thought. *Why be so obsessed about food food food? This is* much *healthier. Now I can free up my mind to embrace other, more important things. Now, I'm really going to find myself.*

"*Kim, I really* didn't appreciate the way you and Will sat in the back of our monthly CE yesterday and laughed," Melissa spat.

"Honestly, I don't know what you're talking about," I lied. "Just because one of us happens to smile doesn't mean we're laughing at anyone."

Will was the only male weight loss counselor in our center. He was a good guy who needed a job. Edie JeJeune was easy work he could do while sitting in a chair. He got a kick out of his clients. He was an engaging person who enjoyed engaging other people, too. Will was short, stout, bearded, sarcastic, and pure hearted. He was in his thirties, still finding himself, had a sonorous voice, and told dirty jokes without apology. His clients were as fanatically loyal to him as mine were to me. Will and I became fast friends at Edie.

Obviously, Melissa had her eye on us during a recent CE. Some weight loss counselors from a neighboring center had joined us for the training session. A male counselor with ginger hair was sporting a number of stickers and clownish colored ribbons on the front of his crisp striped shirt. They were awards, along with trainer Nancy's praise of *guh ee-yud!*, for correct answers to her questions.

"Look at 'im," Will said quietly, leaning in toward my ear. "He's sitting there beaming like friggin' Howdy Doody because his shirt's covered in a bunch of scratch 'n' sniff stickers. Where do these trippin' robots *come* from, anyway?"

I gave him a little nudge in the arm to shut him up. The move failed.

"Oh god, I cannot *stand* this Nancy broad," he exhaled. "I used to think I'd screw anything in a skirt at least once but you couldn't get me near *that*. You'd probably have to pause halfway through to wind her back up."

"Shh!" I kept my head down and focused my eyes on the worksheet in my hands. I attempted to mask a laugh by passing it off as a sudden cough, a speck of dust caught at the back of my throat.

Will used to refer to the gals of Edie JeJeune corporate as The Stepford Wives. He didn't believe these women were fashioned of true flesh and blood. His best guess: a realistic polymer facsimile. They all sounded the same. Even in the most informal situations, everything they said seemed eerily scripted. Even when speaking of unpleasant things, their delivery had that same energetic, voiceover-perfect cadence, and they always smiled. They adjusted the angles of their eyebrows ever-so-slightly to convey different emotions, but they never frowned outright. Will loathed them, and he had zero respect for anyone who aspired to be like them.

"I'm not sure I believe you," Melissa said, standing with her arms folded. "It seemed to me you and Will were having a pretty good time during Nancy's lecture."

"Melissa, what are you saying?" I made an earnest face. "Melissa, do you think Nancy's lectures are *unenjoyable*?" I feigned mild outrage. "You're the center manager! Even if you think Nancy's classes *are* boring, Melissa, you really shouldn't be admitting it!"

"No!" she squeaked, her eyes darting toward her open office door. "That is not"—she drew closer to me and lowered her voice"—that is *not* what I'm saying, OK? Forget it, there's really no time for this conversation now anyway. I just signed up two new clients and I'm putting them on your book. Come out and I'll introduce you."

I followed Melissa to the lobby, where two women were waiting side-by-side in folding chairs. As we approached, they stood.

I couldn't believe my eyes.

"Kim, I'd like you to meet Jeannie and Aurora. They're

sisters. I know it's a little unusual, but they're going to be seeing you together from week to week, since they're both doing the program and they live in the same house. A two-for-one deal."

Jeannie and Aurora were long and slender, five-foot-nine. Aurora had luminescent hair the color of cherry wood, porcelain skin, bright green cat's eyes, and high cheekbones. Jeannie had platinum blond hair falling in big, soft waves over her shoulders, a childlike, heart-shaped face, and a golden tan. Jeannie's legs were largely bared in short-shorts, and I noted that her inner thighs didn't touch. I gave both women a kind welcome and ushered them into my office. I had their files open before my ass even hit the chair. *What kind of goal weights could Melissa possibly have calculated for these two?*

"We're dancers," Jeannie volunteered.

"Oh!" I said pleasantly, then with great nonchalance, "Ballroom? Exotic?" I already sensed it was the latter, but I meant to put them at ease.

"We're strippers," Aurora clarified, correctly trusting that I'd be unfazed.

"Do you work across the street at Max's Harem?" I asked cheerfully.

They nodded in unison, seeming to relax. "And sometimes at Manny's in Trevose," added Jeannie.

"We need to get a little weight off. Some of my best costumes are getting a tad tight, and I'm not about to let them out," Aurora said. "I have some beautiful belly-dancing costumes that I had custom made. They cost me a fortune and I'll be damned if I won't fit into them."

"It's probably the alcohol." Jeannie's voice was high and soft, like a little girl's. "But we were just in the liquor store down the street and we found a low-calorie red wine. Is that OK while we're doing Edie?"

I shook my head and mumbled something apologetically negative as I flipped through their files to check their weight loss goals. Jeannie had 6 pounds to lose. Aurora's goal was 7.

"Melissa," I said as I stormed into her office after Jeannie and Aurora departed with their bags of as-yet-unexamined food. "You've got to be kidding me. They don't have an ounce of fat *on* them to lose!"

She swiveled around in her chair as I entered and pushed at the air with her palms, as though she was expecting me and had her argument ready.

"Technically, we can enroll them as long as they have weight to lose, and they do. According to the Edie JeJeune height and weight charts, they're both a few pounds above the lowest weight in their range."

I folded my arms and kinked a corner of my mouth. "This is so wrong. And you know it. They have no business being here. You should have turned them away!"

Melissa shrugged. "Technically, they have every right. They might have smaller goals than most of our clients, but who are we to discriminate?"

"If you had any morality about you whatsoever, you'd refuse to enroll them," I said bitterly. "Let me guess—there's a manager's sales contest this month, right?"

She was about to say something but I turned and stalked out, grumbling the word "disgusting" under my breath. I heard her call my name but didn't turn back. I went straight to the stockroom, grabbed a brand-new box of peanut butter bars from the shelf, and slammed it against the floor with all my might. Then I leaned over and tore the side off the box, pulled out a bar, ripped it open, and took a passionate bite. Lily, the receptionist, was roused from her post and peeked around the edge of the door frame. "Ooh, snack time!" she sing-songed, and she plunged a hand into the box.

Melissa decided to do something exciting and new.

In lieu of our traditional CE sessions with Nancy, we weight loss counselors were given the opportunity to make our own presentations to our co-workers.

"It can be about anything you want," Melissa said, "as long as you can somehow apply it to Edie JeJeune."

The first to volunteer was Renay, who was going to college to become a physical education teacher. She taught us about target heart rates and showed us some basic stretching exercises we could share with our clients.

I volunteered to teach the second session.

Just two months earlier, I had attended a free seminar in an empty retail space three doors down from Edie JeJeune. A husband-and-wife team spoke about what they called wishcraft. They proposed that if you act as if you already *are* the person you want to be, all the resources you need to truly become that person will find you.

The whole concept excited me deeply. I'd suspected as much. I'd even given the idea some spotty trial runs. But I wanted to learn more.

"Most of us think in terms of first taking *actions* in order to transform ourselves," said the woman. "Then through those actions, we expect to obtain certain objects or qualities, so that the end result is, we become who we wanted to be. Do, have, be. That's the order we're accustomed to."

The words *DO HAVE BE* were written on a chalkboard at the head of the room. The woman took a piece of chalk in her fingers and struck them out.

"There's a better way," she said. Then she wrote *BE DO HAVE*.

"Let's say you aspire to be the office manager at your workplace, but right now, you're just the receptionist. You need to start thinking and acting as if you're already a manager," she said.

I briefly imagined myself with Melissa's job, and a wave of nausea passed through me.

"Now, we don't mean that you should walk into the manager's office on Monday morning, take over his desk, and make everyone think you've lost your mind," the man said, and the room tittered. "But you can start, for example, by dressing the way a manager would dress. When you get up in the morning, dress a *manager,* not a receptionist."

His wife nodded vigorously. "Yes," she agreed, "step into the role of the manager in your mind. *Believe* that you are a manager. Start doing the kinds of things a manager would do, like reading industry publications and volunteering for more responsibility."

"If you walk into the office every day looking the part of a manager and carrying yourself like one, believe me — you won't stay a receptionist for long," her husband assured us. "People will assume you're management material, and that job *will* come to you."

Act like the person you want to be, and the world will buy it. Ah yes, I understood this! This was what made it possible for me to perform in plays and musicals in community theater as a kid, when I felt like such a reject at school. I'd proven to myself I was capable of pretending to be braver and bolder than I really was.

Do-have-be versus be-do-have.

The day after the free seminar, I purchased my very first appointment calendar. The kind a famous author would have. I started setting goals for myself, breaking them down into tiny baby steps. I was incorporating practical action into the concept of Be Do Have. I was referring to myself as "a writer," even if nobody ever read the stories I scribbled into dog-eared notebooks at three a.m. Being a writer was my dearest and most stubborn childhood dream. Within a month I had my first writing assignment for a local music magazine. Another month later, I wrote the cover story for the next issue.

Standing before my fellow white coats in the Edie training room, I used the easel, the marker, and the jumbo flip chart to explain being, doing, and having. I shared my own surprisingly quick success stories from recent weeks.

Melissa stood in the back, listening with the corner of a file folder pressed against her mouth. About halfway through the presentation, she interrupted and said, "Okay okay, but how does this relate to *Edie JeJeune*?"

"Here's how." I was prepared for just such a question. "Remember last month when Melissa introduced the sales contest for the motivational tapes?"

My pupils nodded.

"We all know how hard it is to move those things. They're *way* too expensive and people really aren't convinced they need them."

From the corner of my sight, I detected a dissatisfied shift in Melissa's posture. I went on.

"I had clients I was reminding every week for six months to buy those stupid tapes, and I was convinced they'd keep putting it off for eternity.

"Then, I took six sets of tapes and put them in my office. I stacked them right on my desk, where I could see them, and I became completely convinced that I could move them. I was going to *be* the kind of person who sold those tapes effortlessly. And I looked at what I could concretely *do* to make that a reality. At the beginning of every shift, I checked the files of all the clients on my book for that day, and made a mental note of which ones hadn't purchased the tapes yet. I *believed* that this time, they would actually walk out with them—no more excuses. I also forced myself to talk about the tapes even though I'm usually terrified to do it because I don't want my clients getting pissed off at me for being such a shameless saleswoman. But I pushed past that fear, remembering that I *am* the kind of woman people buy tapes from. And guess what? I sold six sets of tapes in one week. Unheard of, right? I mean, really—who sells six sets of those tapes in a week?"

Some gasped. Everyone nodded in agreement.

"And now, I *have* the commission money in the bank. See that? Be, do, have." Quickly I shifted gears again and added, "But it doesn't matter what your goal is. You can achieve anything you set your mind to. You can be anyone you want to be. Just believe that you already are." I continued my presentation without another mention of Edie JeJeune. I'd paid my lip service.

After my closing words, my co-workers applauded. Some approached me afterward and congratulated me on a great presentation. Then we mingled around a refreshment table.

Evelyn, our center's assistant manager, pulled me aside.

"Kim, that was incredibly moving. I want you to know, you really changed my life tonight."

"Wow. Really? I . . . I did?"

"Thanks to you, I've made up my mind. I'm not staying at Edie JeJeune anymore. I'm going back to school to do what I *really* want to do. I want to be a nutritionist."

"Evelyn, that's great!" I squealed.

"Yeah! Yeah, I know!" Evelyn beamed. "You made me

realize I gave up too soon. I let myself get overwhelmed. But if I take fewer classes at a time, I'll be able to manage it better. I'll get there slowly, but still, eventually I'll get there. I *will* be a practicing nutritionist. I can see it in my mind's eye, and it's right. I mean, what am I doing here?" Evelyn looked around for Melissa, and not seeing her, continued. "What we do here is totally bogus. There are so many holes in this approach. Besides, this isn't how I used to picture my life. I'm giving my two weeks' notice to Melissa tomorrow. Thank you so much for everything."

As I was pulling on my coat to leave for the evening, Melissa called me into her office.

"I can't believe it! She quit!"

Already? I thought. *I could've sworn Evelyn said she was giving her notice tomorrow, not tonight.* I decided the best strategy was to maintain a blank look and let Melissa keep talking, which she did.

"Two minutes ago, DeeDee walked into this office and resigned. And she said it was because of *your* little class!"

DeeDee was another weight loss counselor. I tried hard not to let a smile creep across my face and remained silent.

"She was sooooooo inspired, she realized she wasn't doing what she loves here at Edie, and decided to go work in a hospital with . . . I don't know, *kids* or something!"

I shrugged. Melissa's voice grew louder.

"Well, what do you have to say for yourself, Kim Brittingham?!"

I paused, with a look of genuine bewilderment dripping down my face and off the point of my chin. "I don't know. I guess my presentation was pretty good."

"Ugh!" Melissa fell back into her chair, as though she was completely exasperated. But at the same time, I sensed some purposeful comedy in the act.

It's ironic that Melissa was the person who first forced me to look for a way to tie together Edie JeJeune and my newfound "be do have" philosophy of living. Ironic indeed, because the more I allowed the two streams to cross in my mind, the more I came to hate everything Edie JeJeune stood for.

I realized that Edie JeJeune wanted people to believe they had to *do* her diet first in order to *have* thinner bodies so they could then *be* beautiful. Beautiful, or interesting, or likable, or lovable.

I dared to imagine it the other way around. What if people could just *be* beautiful, important, interesting, and lovable, and then *do* things to support a long life of being all those things—then they would *have* it all. What if my clients and I just... *were* the people we wanted to be already? Not by virtue of losing weight, but simply by *deciding* it? What if we *could* just put the "be" first, without waiting for Edie JeJeune's—or society's—permission?

It made me sad to know that so many of my clients— smart people, creative people; loving parents, curious students; people with much to give, with ideas, with hearts and minds—did not see how wonderful and complete they already were. They didn't see themselves the way I saw them. They moved through life as *too-fat people*. People too fat to be anything *but* fat people, until they were thin people, and *then* they'd begin to live. When the scale gave them the thumbs-up, they'd claim their identity. Then, they'd dare to *be* somebody. Until then, the only dream they entitled themselves to was the dream of being thinner. Even more disturbing to me were the people who believed themselves to be fat but weren't.

At Edie, we were routinely taught to deal with a client's flagging enthusiasm by bringing him or her back to the reasons he or she signed up in the first place. When an Edie salesperson enrolled a new client, he or she made notes in the file of very specific things the client mentioned in the intake interview. Then weight loss counselors like me could refer back to those early motivators to rekindle commitment to the Edie JeJeune program. Remember, Carol, how you wanted to show up at your twenty-five-year high school reunion looking even better than you did at seventeen?

I was growing less comfortable using this tactic. In our attempts to motivate our clients, it seemed we were actually just promoting the idea of putting off life until thinness.

I had a client, Marie, who'd begun fantasizing about returning to diving, maybe even coaching young divers. She'd been a diving champion in high school. Suddenly her eight-year-old daughter was showing an interest, as well as her mother's natural ability. The little girl was making remarks like, "Mommy, I wish I could see *you* dive."

It broke Marie's heart. She'd managed to stay out of a bathing suit for ten years. She was ashamed of her body, which was at least sixty pounds heavier than it had been when she graduated high school. She told me, "I'd never stand on a diving board in front of other people in a bathing suit. Not even in front of children. It would be like standing up on a stage with a spotlight on my fat!"

Practicing the Edie JeJeune method of motivation, I told Marie to imagine herself *finally thinner,* climbing that ladder, stepping lightly to the end of the diving board, looking up at her daughter waving from the opposite end of the pool, and then making a gentle arc through the air before slicing almost noiselessly through the turquoise water.

Over time, Marie grew frustrated and impatient. She

wanted to dive again *now,* but as she saw it, her fat stood in her way. And she hated herself for *getting* so fat. It was her fault she had to wait so many years to dive again—she'd *let* herself go to pot. She had no one else to blame.

Sometimes there'd be a moment, a flicker, just before Marie gave in to a "forbidden" food, when she'd think, *Well, I'm so far from my goal weight anyway. Happiness is probably still years in the future. I can't expect myself to be miserable for* that *long. At least I can give myself a* minute *of pleasure now in the form of this cinnamon bun.* Afterward, she'd feel remorse for having set herself back *yet again,* one step further away from the dream. And she'd blame herself for her grand failures in life: her fatness, her lack of willpower. And she was still aching to dive; that hadn't gone away. And if she couldn't even lose weight for the sake of her own child, that meant she was a horrible, horrible human being. A big zero.

Marie was so miserable.

I wish I could go back in time and recounsel Marie. I would tell her to put a bathing suit on whatever body she had now and take a dive *today*. I would encourage her to let go of the embarrassment of being seen in a bathing suit, of caring what other people thought about her body. If only she could become immune to other people's opinions, she could finally set her soul free and dive *that very day,* and experience the joy of it immediately. Instead, she might die tomorrow, of any accidental cause, and would have wasted the gift of life beating herself up for failing to be thin "enough." She'd have spent her adult life dieting, putting off everything else. Instead of leaving her daughter with the enduring memory of her mother as a breathtaking diver and loving teacher, Marie was impressing upon her observant child a very different lesson.

But as Marie's "weight loss counselor"—as *anyone's* weight loss counselor—I was a total fraud.

I was no longer an exemplary adherent to the Edie Je-Jeune weight loss program. About two months into it, I'd become uncontrollable around peanut butter and any food containing peanut butter. I was using my lunch hour to skedaddle across the parking lot to the supermarket, where I made a beeline for the Reese's Peanut Butter Cups shaped like pumpkins (then later, Christmas trees, hearts, Easter eggs). I always bought two. I imagined justifying myself to the other customers in the express checkout line, "One for now, and one for *later*." Even though I always ate them one after the other, quickly, in my office with the door closed.

Plus, Will and I had taken to visiting White Castle after the night shift. When the last client was sent bobbing toward her car with her overstuffed bags of Edie's Eaties, we'd cast off our white coats into our respective office doorways, rush the exit, and, minutes later, roll through the White Castle drive-through. We'd park just outside the white sphere of an overhead light, and wolf down dozens of White Castle's trademark miniburgers in Will's front seat. They were never my favorite burgers in the world. The meat patties appeared more gray than brown, and that bothered me. Besides, there was something creepy about the fact that each patty had been punched by a perfect series of tiny holes. Just a little *too* similar to bloated paper. But at the time, I couldn't get enough of them.

I was sitting in my office doing paperwork when Melissa knocked on my door.

"Kim, I thought you should know, Will has just been fired."

"Huh?"

"He was eating Edie's Eaties and dumping them in the trash can outside the back door. Did you know about this?"

I sat there frowning, saying nothing for a moment while I tried to make sense of what I was hearing. "Know about it? No, I — wait, what do you mean, he was eating Edie's Eaties? Like what?"

"Come see for yourself!"

Melissa took off down the long hallway of counselors' offices and I followed on her heels. She threw open the door to the alley where our trash was placed and collected every night. An aluminum garbage can stood just beside the door and she lifted its lid.

"Look!"

Inside were dozens of discarded wrappers, cardboard boxes, and microwave trays of Edie's Eaties, licked clean. This wasn't limited to the typical array of frequently "damaged" foods, like peanut butter bars or little packets of granola, or cans of ready-to-eat tuna salad. There were remnants of once-frozen dinner entrées, deflated salad dressing packets, even flat, formerly vacuum-sealed plastic pouches for pot roast and congealed unheated gravy.

Pot roast? I exclaimed — to myself, not to Melissa. *He was eating the* pot roast?

I must've worn such a look of genuine revulsion that it was immediately clear to Melissa that I knew nothing of Will's ongoing food theft.

"He's been doing it for weeks!" she said, slamming the lid back on the garbage can.

Later, in the parking lot outside of White Castle, Will confessed, "I don't know *what* I was doin'." He was agitated. "It's not like the food is that great. Maybe subconsciously, I was just trying to stick it to Edie."

One afternoon on my way to Edie JeJeune, I paused at

a red light on Roosevelt Boulevard. Someone had dropped their lunch in the intersection. The flattened remains of a ham-and-Swiss hoagie caught the attention of two pigeons and they swooped down to peck at it. They had only a moment as the light was changing, before traffic began its slow surge across the asphalt sea. My eyes stayed on the birds as they weighed the situation. I could read their thoughts through their tiny, twitching gray eyes. They glanced rapidly between the edible lump and two lanes of gunning cars: *Food or death?* Tires rolled forward. This wasn't an easy decision. Their necks twisted wildly from left to right. *Food or death? Food or death?* Sunlight glanced off a fender. One bird touched his beak tentatively to the compressed Italian roll. Were these pigeons actually willing to die for a taste of a trodden sandwich? Traffic bore down on them. They fluttered expertly into the air on a swift diagonal and were gone.

I rested one hand over the other on the steering wheel and ruminated. *All living things need food. All living things want food. Food has a powerful pull. And that's natural, isn't it?* I thought about my parents' dog, Patches. They often neglected to feed him. They didn't want to spend money on dog food. Sometimes I took pity on him, bought cases of dog food, and stacked them in the corner of the kitchen and hoped someone would be motivated to open one and dump its contents into a bowl. He wasn't my dog, but I couldn't stand to see him suffer. My mother used to get pissed off when Patches ate the soap right out of the bathtub. Sometimes he'd turn over the wastebasket and gnaw at my mother's discarded feminine products. He simply wasn't getting fed.

Later, as yet another client sat in my office and bemoaned her own frailty of character for cheating on a diet,

I wondered if what we were doing at Edie JeJeune was completely unnatural.

We were the weight loss counselors. We were the guiding, front-line force for this savior of a weight loss plan. In our white coats we represented knowledge, health, fresh air, help, light, hope.

But we stole and gorged in private, and we stole and gorged in subversive giggling circles.

Some of us did it on behalf of our clients. If we sensed that Edie JeJeune was taking them for a ride but we didn't quite know how to save them, at least we could deplete Edie's snack bar stock in a feeble, misguided attempt at "screw you."

For some of us, it was a subconscious reflex, an attempt to bring balance to the constant barrage of "eat this, not that" coming at us from the corporation and parroted from our guilty mouths to the gullible ears of our clients. We may not have had enough self-awareness and clarity to verbalize it, but many of us had grown weary of the ceaseless chatter about *every single morsel* that went into our mouths, our clients' mouths. We sought equilibrium at the other extreme, in cases of Edie's Eaties peanut butter bars. We *needed* at times not to care at all. We *needed* to completely lose count.

It's ironic that I once viewed the Edie JeJeune weight loss program as an effective way to avoid obsessing over food, when actually, Edie JeJeune helped *create* a food obsession. In at least one way, Edie JeJeune was no different from every other diet I've tried — Weight Watchers, Nutrisystem, Richard Simmons's Deal-A-Meal. By limiting my food choices in an effort to lose weight, I became obsessed with all the foods I believed I couldn't have. After a few short weeks on any given weight loss program, I felt an unbearable urge to buy huge quantities of fattening foods and devour them from inside a silent sphere where I saw nothing, tasted nothing, thought of nothing.

There was definitely an aspect of rebellion in those moments — my mind and body breaking free from the restrictions I placed upon it and running amok. To hell with you, Weight Watchers. To hell with you, too, Nutrisystem. Bite me, Edie JeJeune. I'll eat what I want.

Sometimes I recognized this truculent teenager in my fellow weight loss counselors. The newly hired ones went on the Edie JeJeune diet in earnest. They wanted to be good employees, good counselors. They wanted to make people healthier, they wanted to set an example, walk the walk. But sooner or later, they'd be found pulling a handful of peanut butter bars from an open box in the stockroom and slipping away with them to their office. Deep inside, they were tired of being told "no."

Later in life, I looked back and realized that my overeating was more than just a foot-stomping little girl on a tantrum told she couldn't have what she wanted exactly when she wanted it. And it had nothing to do with being a weak-willed pansy, either, failing to pull myself up by the bootstraps.

When I restricted and preplanned my eating, there was something happening at my core that was more unconscious than revolt. I thought about those pigeons. I thought about how longing for food is as authentic to living things as the drive to reproduce. Longing for food is an ancient and fundamental thing. Is it any wonder that when we begin to toy with our food (and, by extension, our own heads), we have a strong reaction? That we become covetous of food? That we obsess? We're taught to believe that the ability to resist food is at once angelic and the calling card of the agile modern warrior. It is neither. It's just plain messed up. It's not what we're meant to do. I believe we're meant to say yes to food, so that we'll become convinced of its abundance, and thus be able to think about something else.

I do believe that every time I went on a diet, an ages-old, biologically based rebellion was launched. However, there was another level of diet rejection that dwelled a little closer to the surface of my consciousness, and it was the nuclear core of fed-uppedness that fueled certain binges. It was a fundamental refusal to believe I was undeserving of happiness just the way I was.

I think there's a fighter inside me, maybe inside all of us, whose sole purpose is to defend us against enemies—especially those enemies masquerading as friends. Maybe this fighter is wiser than the other parts of us, and recognizes a line of bullshit more readily. Maybe this rabid defender of our well-being is trying to communicate with us through our binges.

Maybe, just as we begin to get hypnotized by the "yes you can!" and "yes you should" language of diets, the inner fighter struggles to be heard. *Don't let them slap you on the wrist and tell you you're a bad girl for eating. Don't buy in to the idea that strong, successful people must always prove their strength by winning a battle over food and/or focusing their energy on sculpting a particular kind of body. And don't let them tell you to "come back later" for acceptance. You're just as valuable a human being now as you might be fifty pounds from now. Accept no other message!*

Maybe the less-sophisticated parts of ourselves feel guilty for having such an angry person inside of us, so we eat. Or maybe those coarser parts of ourselves reject the enemy of The Diet by eating. It's a clumsy reaction, but the healthier sentiment is in there, somewhere. *I will not*

*let you shame me for eating. I will not allow you to tell me
I'm undeserving of happiness just because I don't meet your
physical standards. Who the hell are you to set the standard
anyway?*

"*I don't know* what to do." Helen Witter wept, dropping
her head onto her crossed arms. "My husband is out of
work. My daughter hasn't uttered a word since her rape.
We just got our second eviction notice from our landlord.
And the doctor says if I don't get this weight under control, I'm going to wind up dead within a couple of years.
I don't know what else to do, Kim. I try and try, but the
scale isn't moving! And I didn't deviate from the plan once
this week, not once! Except for two Girl Scout cookies from
my neighbor, I stuck to Edie to the letter! What can I do?"

*Well, Helen, I can't say I'm completely surprised. After
all, if you want to be successful on the Edie JeJeune program,
you need to use* all *the tools available to you. And I see here
in your file that you haven't purchased the motivational tapes
yet. It sounds like you're finally ready to take them home
with you this week. Shall I put those on your credit card, or
would you like to pay cash?*

I reached out and took Helen's hand.

"It's all right, Helen," I said softly. Then I closed my office door. "I know you're concerned about your health. But
it sounds like you have a lot going on right now, and I
wouldn't blame you if your focus was on something other
than your weight. And I don't necessarily think it's true
that you're going to drop dead in two years, even if you
stay this weight. Your doctor's just trying to scare you."

I didn't have the answer for why Helen wasn't losing
weight. I couldn't possibly know if changing the way she
ate would even affect her weight. Maybe it wouldn't. I was

just an Edie JeJeune weight loss counselor. I didn't even have a college degree.

I remember wishing I had a crystal ball that would show me exactly what Helen should eat, and in just what quantities, and how often, in order for her to live the longest, healthiest, happiest life possible. But nobody had that resource, nobody. And besides, even if I did, and Helen followed my advice with absolute precision, who's to say that diet wouldn't make her crazy? Maybe it would consist of all the foods she hates, and she'd find it impossible to stick with.

I did the best I could with what I had.

"Listen, Helen. If you can't afford this food anymore, here's an idea. Do you still have all your Edie JeJeune menus?"

She nodded.

"Go to the supermarket and buy some canned tuna, get some frozen dinners, get some cereal. Just try duplicating the kinds of meals that were on Edie's plan, and be sure to pay attention to portion size. You've been doing this long enough to know how to eat."

After Helen left, I wrote up a letter of resignation and placed it face-up on Melissa's desk.

She appeared at my door moments later, holding it in her hand.

"I don't believe this. I was going to fire you today."

I smiled at her and put on my coat. "Sorry to disappoint."

"When Nancy was visiting the center the other day, she overheard you at the front desk with your client. You used the word 'they' in referring to Edie JeJeune. That's grounds for dismissal."

I paused for a second, wondering what the hell she was talking about.

"What do you mean, 'they'?"

"When you work for Edie JeJeune, you're part of a team. You used the word 'they' with your client as if *you* were separate from *Edie*. The woman was asking for some kind of special arrangement and you told her, 'I'll see what *they* say.' But your choice of words gives away your lack of loyalty to Edie. You should've said 'we.' Like 'We'll see what *we* can do.' When you're with Edie, you have to stand behind her one hundred percent."

I made it a point to look at her like she was utterly ridiculous. "Uh-huh. I see." I pulled my shoulder bag over my head. "Well, good luck with that, comrade." I left my office and started toward the exit.

Here's the saddest part. What I learned at Edie JeJeune, and even the lessons of the friendly couple preaching be-do-have in a shopping center, proved slippery to a weight-obsessed American girl like me. In the coming years, I would forget. A certain number on the scale might send me into high alert and I'd think, *Oh God, I can't afford to get any fatter than this. I just can't.* Once again, I'd tinker with my food intake. I'd *try* to lose weight. I'd trust and pay other diet peddlers, whose sole reason for existing was to turn a profit, to feed me a system that would "fix" me, *save* me. And I'd lose weight. And then I'd gain it back again, plus more.

It was strange. Like blacking out for years at a time in favor of visions of thinness. I'd forget that my dreams were possible at any size. I'd forget *my* power and let the diet pushers, and everybody else who'd been brainwashed by them, have power over *me*.

But those revelations from my Edie JeJeune days planted a valuable seed. The things I knew, but subconsciously

chose to look away from, popped up again in other set-
tings. They tapped me on the shoulder and said, *Pssst,
hey — remember us?* Sometimes I'd turn to look and it was
as though I'd *never seen them before.* Brainwashed again.
But each time I was willing to turn and look, the truth
settled in more deeply. The seeds took root. I embraced my
fat body. I ran toward all my gorgeous possibility.

CAN'T STAND THE FARM STAND

When I was a kid, I didn't take too kindly to being served farm-fresh fruits or vegetables.

I hated almost all fresh produce. To me, fresh vegetables tasted like dirt and water. And fruit tasted like watered-down Kool-Aid, with just a *pinch* of dirt.

I lapped up plates of canned green beans, canned peas, and canned corn—highly salted, sopping soft, and slightly metallic tasting. But I wouldn't touch a fresh vegetable.

It wasn't in my mother's routine to serve a predinner salad. Which was a good thing, because I detested tossed salad. To me it looked like garbage—akin to rinds and onion skins, like something you'd push into soggy piles in the kitchen sink and throw into the trash bag with a splat.

Once my mother brought home a bag of green beans from the supermarket. I still remember the light from the window above the kitchen sink filtered through the semi-transparent plastic bag on the counter, weighted down by two cups of long green Grinch fingers in the bottom. She boiled them and served them up.

"They're *hard,*" I grimaced. I was disturbed by the snap when my molars came down on the bean. The skin required too much chewing. This foreign thing didn't belong in my mouth.

"*Blech*!" I noised, spitting half-chewed bean into my napkin. "It tastes like it's been in the ground." My mother rolled her eyes and shrugged in resignation. "Because it *has* been, Kim."

Some nights as we sat down to eat, my mother's mouth turned up into an impish smile as she announced in a soft voice, "And after dinner, we're going to have a *treat*!"

The faces of my little brother and baby sister lit up, and my brother bellowed hopefully, "Fruit cocktail?!"

My mother nodded vigorously and a cheer went up. She didn't have to look at my face to know what it said. "Don't worry," she added dryly. "I made some chocolate pudding for you."

The following year, my mother had an epiphany. She decided I should be eating more fruit, so she began packing an apple with my daily school lunch.

"You like apple juice," she reminded me. "So why won't you eat an apple?"

"It's not the same," I whined. "And I don't like the skin. It feels like wet cardboard between my teeth."

"Well, what if I peel the skin off and cut the apple up for you?"

I wasn't enthusiastic, but my mother plowed ahead anyway.

"That's what I'll do," she decided. "Tomorrow I'll put some peeled apple slices in a little sandwich bag and pack it in your lunchbox."

By lunchtime, the apple slices were soft and starting to brown. I observed that they looked more like potato chips than apple slices, and wished they were. The apple slices were mushy, a little gritty against my back teeth, kind of slimy.

I told my mother they were tasteless, and she argued that apples were sweet and that I liked sweet things. But to my over-sugared tongue—coated with many seasons' worth of Reese's Peanut Butter Cups and oily cheap chocolate wrapped in foil and molded like bunnies and Santas and little footballs; a tongue painted thick with creamy white filling; melted Fudgsicle juice; and the dust of hundreds of Chips Ahoy—all fruit tasted like tap water.

When I was in my early twenties, I moved out of my parents' house and into a sparse, roach-ridden apartment in Philadelphia that I decorated with cheap party supplies for Chinese New Year and furniture abandoned on curbs or near Dumpsters. It was my first home, my first taste of total independence, and everything I did was my call. And when I shopped for my very own groceries, I bought canned vegetables and no fruit at all.

My friend Parvin, however, lived differently. She was a creative cook who experienced her true power while presiding over a stove. She was born in Iran, where each meal was prepared from fresh ingredients purchased in the village that same day. It wasn't her way to reach for a can or a box of instant anything. She shopped for raw ingredients and performed culinary sculpture, shaping dishes with herbs and spices and inspired combinations. I was a regular visitor to her apartment and benefited from her uncontrollable urge to cook when any pair of elbows hit her kitchen table. I used to joke that even with "nothing in the house," she could whip up a gourmet meal with little more than a jar of mustard, a three-year-old powdered gravy packet, and a single petrified raisin found at the bottom of the pantry. She made the simplest things magical. Parvin was the first person to make me realize that fruits and vegetables could actually be delicious.

There was a produce stand around the corner from that first crappy apartment of mine. Besides a pizza parlor, it was the commercial establishment nearest my front door. It was actually called Kim's.

Parvin loved Kim's. Often when she came to pick me up for dinner at her place, we stopped at Kim's so she could shop for the meal. The first couple of times I loped behind her like a bored child, blind to the splendor around me. All I could see was a maze of crates packed with stuff that'd been pulled out of dirt. I couldn't relate to Parvin's gasps of ecstasy as she paused at mountains of sweet Jersey corn and lovingly peeled away a supple green leaf to reveal its virginal, pearly white kernels. I didn't understand the appeal of fondling rich purple plums, of dirtying one's hands to stroke a heap of clay-colored yams.

All I understood was that the finished product, at Parvin's enchanted hands, was scrumptious.

Back then, I was only interested in fruits and vegetables insofar as they could help me lose weight. It seemed every diet I'd ever been on wanted to *gag* you with them—five, six servings a *day*! I remember the Weight Watchers food diary and all the tiny boxes one had to check off each day, each one representing one unit of a particular type of food. It was a real struggle for me to fill in all five or six of the fruit-and-veg circles every day. I was lucky if I filled in one, and that was usually for orange juice.

After a while I began to suspect that this fruit-and-vegetable thing was just some nutritional mumbo-jumbo, that it wouldn't actually help me lose *weight* any faster—thus, why bother? And I felt there was something about forcing a piece of fruit down my throat that made me think the fruit itself might actually be promoting my weight loss. That somehow, nature would be fair with me, balance things out—if I was willing to not only forgo my favorite sugary treats for months at a time but *also* to take on the *additional* torture of ingesting fruits and vegetables, somehow, I would lose weight faster. The amount of my sacrifice, the intensity of my displeasure, would equal my reward.

Eventually, I reasoned I'd probably reach my goal sooner if I *didn't* eat all those tiresome fruits and vegetables, because after all, it was less food, and therefore fewer calories.

"I don't know what to *do* with these things," I said, trailing Parvin through the produce section at the supermarket.

"What do you mean, you don't know what to do with them? You *cook* them. Or you chop them up and eat them raw, depending on what it is. Didn't you ever watch your mom cook when you were a kid?"

"My mom didn't cook stuff like this." I frowned, picking up an alien-looking thing the earth had spewed on a particularly painful hiccup. "Like, what the heck is *this*?"

"It's jicama," Parvin replied. "Well, what *did* your mother cook? Are you saying she never made a vegetable?" She made a sweeping gesture over several aisles of farmed foods.

"Not like *these*."

My mother's meals are etched into my memory with eerie clarity. Certain things were always, reliably paired with certain other things.

Like frozen corn dogs with Tater Tots.

Hot dogs with canned chili-and-beans spooned on top and then, oddly enough, *separate* canned baked beans served on the side.

Spaghetti and meatballs.

Meatloaf with instant mashed potatoes—the kind

made from snowy flakes out of a red cardboard box — and canned green beans.

Pork chops with canned peas and scalloped potatoes from a box.

"All right, we'll start with one thing." Parvin approached a slanted table plentiful with funny little green pumpkins. She dropped two into a thin plastic bag and plopped them into her shopping cart. "When we get back to my place, I'm going to show you how I make these. It's so simple. They're delicious steamed, with just a little butter."

"What are they?"

"Do you like sweet potatoes?" she asked. I nodded.

"Then you'll love these. They're acorn squash."

Parvin taught me how to stick an acorn squash under the tap and wash off the dirt, then once clean, how to cut it in half, scoop out the seeds with a teaspoon, and stick it upside-down inside a steamer. Finally, she melted modest pats of butter inside the bowl-like vegetables and we ate them. The sweet, tender meat pulled away from the outer skin easily, one spoonful at a time.

"Wow," I mumbled, mouth half full. "This is amazing."

Parvin nodded. "Mm-hm. And Kimmy, you can melt cheese over these, or you can add a dollop of sour cream or yogurt in the center. And that was pretty easy to make, right?"

I don't think Parvin knew what she was doing when she chose that acorn squash, but it was an amazing stroke of fate. My introduction to preparing and eating fresh vegetables involved something *sweet* — the perfect buffer between a lifelong diet of candy bars, snack cakes, and ice cream and this new world of fresh produce. It turned out to be just the right thing to lure me a little bit closer to the veggie wagon.

There'd been something satisfying and crafty about preparing the squash, too. Like making a potholder on a miniature loom or hooking a Snoopy rug, only this was *edible*. And *good for me*. And I *liked* it!

For the first time, I went by myself to Kim's farm stand. I felt so proud bagging my acorn squash and toting it home. I felt like a Renaissance woman, "in the know." Someone highly capable of taking good care of herself. A grown-up with good habits. Habits that walked the walk of a woman intent on living a brisk, well-rounded life. As I rigged up a successful steaming apparatus with a saucepan and colander, I felt competent, ever evolving. I cooked and ate acorn squash twice a week for months. This was *my* vegetable, baby! I was *owning* it!

Soon Parvin introduced me to zucchini, both green and yellow. My repertoire gradually expanded. I started buying fresh lemons and squeezing them over sizzling chicken and tofu. I still wasn't too keen on apples, but I took a daring bite out of a Bosc pear one day and fell in love. One evening as Parvin peeled a clementine during a rerun of *Star Trek*, I warily agreed to put a tiny section of the citrus fruit into my mouth. It smelled wonderful, but I was disgusted by that weird, Creamsicle-colored lichen that clung to the fruit from the inside of the peel. Skeptically, I took the juice-filled, bean-shaped pillow into my mouth and it exploded, cascading pure heaven over my taste buds. Its membrane was much easier to chew than I expected. I asked Parvin for a clementine of my own. She laughed, and I laughed at myself. I was peeling fruit. I was removing its clingy bits, uncomplaining. I was *choosing* this food, choosing it over a Cadbury Caramello bar or a bag of Fritos.

There came a day when I moved away from Philadelphia and Parvin, and settled in New York City. There I explored gourmet shops and the Union Square farmer's market. On autumn jaunts into neighboring New Jersey, I discovered the joys of carving one's jack-o'-lantern from a pumpkin picked directly from the patch. I found a farm with fields of squash and gourds of every variety, sunflowers and apple trees, and established an annual pilgrimage there. They grew acorn squash there, too, and I derived an extraspecial pleasure from cutting them right off the vine. I liked leaving a trailing length of the dry, shriveled vine attached to the squash when I brought it home. There was something beautiful about it in the context of my kitchen, out of its natural environment, but still wearing a short length of kinked vine like a Chinaman's queue, hinting at the delightfully gnarled October field from where it came.

Even now, I find few things more pleasant than riding in a hay wagon, hugging a plump, pretty pumpkin against my faded button-down denim shirt, letting the dried earth crusted within the pumpkin's vertical creases loosen and crumble and smear my clothes brown.

There was a time when I became curious about edible varieties of pumpkin and wanted to learn how to prepare and eat them. I took a cooking class: seven ways to cook pumpkin. My favorite recipe involved carving a lid into a pumpkin and stuffing it with layers of crusty bread, crème fraîche, and Gruyère, baking it for hours and then artfully pulling the meat of the pumpkin away from the outer walls and stirring it into the mix without collapsing the pumpkin itself. The dish is brought to the table served inside the pumpkin with its lid replaced. I find this recipe deeply satisfying, highlighting the innate deliciousness of the vegetable by serving it from within natural packaging;

a pumpkin so beautifully formed and grooved, perfect in its imperfections, swollen and round and warm.

When I served my very first stuffed pumpkin, I realized I'd arrived at a place where I finally understood what Parvin felt when she wandered through a produce market and reacted so sensually to those rows and rows of dirty vegetables heaped in coarse crates.

I still don't like green beans when they're too crisp. I like them steamed ultrasoft, unless they've been doctored in some irresistible way. And there were vegetables to which Parvin introduced me that I ended up disliking, like steamed fennel, *ugh*. I'm still experimenting with different varieties of apples but I have yet to get excited about them, unless they're served on a stick, dipped in caramel, and rolled in chopped peanuts.

I eat more fruits and vegetables now than I ever did as a child, though, and not in the least bit due to a desire to lose weight. I eat some fruits and vegetables because they taste delicious. Often I choose them over junk food I find equally delicious, because I like the way I feel after I eat them. My insides feel cleaner, somehow, when I eat fresh food. And I try to eat organic as often as possible. I started to realize that all those preservatives and pesticides can't possibly be good for me. Sometimes when I think about how many chemicals are in the food I eat, I feel like the walking embalmed. Even so, I don't eat organic food exclusively. I believe you have to make room for every kind of food that calls to you, or it messes with your head.

I make better food choices because I've come to value my *experience* of life more than how I *appear* in this life, or what size my body is at any given point. I value feeling energized, serene, clear, and positive. And I want to feel this way, and stay mobile in these happy states of being, for as long as possible.

And regardless of what size or shape my body may be, no matter how it may change—bigger, smaller, looser, older—I want to be loved just as I am. Me, in my natural packaging, appreciated for the whole that I am, for all the wonderful innate qualities I bring to the table.

BELLY

I used to have a boyfriend who liked to stick his finger into my navel — poke! There was an accompanying sound effect, too: *"Booop!"* Every once in a while, when I felt bloated after a meal and reclined with my big white belly pulled out of my pants, he'd try it. And I'd flinch and instinctively push his hands away.

"God, don't *do* that!" I panicked. "You might pop me!"

The first time I said this, he threw his head back and cackled. *"What?* What do you mean, *pop* you?"

I heard a story once about a man who was so fat that his stomach burst open without warning, unraveling from his bellybutton. It probably isn't true. Nevertheless, I've never forgotten it.

"Where did you hear that?" Ray sounded skeptical, and still deeply amused.

"I don't know," I snapped. "On a . . . like a . . . documentary or something. Just don't do it, okay? I don't want to take any chances."

From that moment on, he abandoned the sound effect. Instead, whenever he poked my navel, he'd exclaim (tunefully), "Don't *pop* meee!"

* * *

I was used to overstuffing myself. To the point where my belly was so full, it seemed to rise into the space of my lungs and I found myself sighing again and again, trying to force sufficient oxygen into my lungs. To the point where the skin around my belly was so distended, it started to pinch and I feared my sides would split. Like two clean, neat incisions traveling rapidly in opposite directions from their opening point. Like a run in a pair of pantyhose.

These were unpleasant sensations. The pressure of all that food inside me switched on my anxiety button, because it made me imagine all the awful things that might be going wrong inside my body, things that might result in sickness or disease. I feared illness, and hospitals, and the thought of long, shiny instruments invading the untouched purity of my insides.

My therapist encouraged me to explore the motivation behind my overstuffing. "Clearly, it's uncomfortable for you," she noted.

"It is!" I affirmed. "It's *scary* when I get like that. Breathing feels like work. I'm afraid I'm going to have a heart attack before I even have a chance to poop all that food out of me. And I'm afraid that my bellybutton will start to unrav—well, yes, it's very uncomfortable."

"So if you do it anyway, the overstuffing must be serving you in some way. What's the payoff?"

The *payoff.* Gee, I never thought of it that way—that if I was repeatedly getting myself into this uncomfortable mess, I must also be getting something *out* of it. But I couldn't find anything positive in the situation. What was wrong with me? Why did I keep signing up for this?

I imagined myself in that tumescent state, sunk low into

the sofa cushions, belly released from the confines of my clothing and bared to the cool air. I saw its swollen whiteness riding high under my breasts, as though I was carrying a girl. Or twin girls. Firm as a basketball. How *was* this serving me?

When my belly is *that full,* it feels like I'm being hugged—from the *inside.* Like someone is putting their arms around me and squeezing like they mean it.

And when I'm *that full,* it feels like someone or something else is "with" me. A presence, a separate entity. I have company.

And being *that full* makes me feel anchored and substantial, like things that are designed to resist blowing over in hurricanes. A Dumpster, maybe. I'm tethered to the earth. I'm no longer vulnerable, nor so easily shifted from one place to another.

Every occasion of overstuffing myself has been a subconscious tug-of-war between wanting to feel *that full* and dreading it.

My belly is an old friend. It's been with me since early adolescence. My belly never dismissed my fears and concerns with ridicule in front of my younger siblings, who'd then sing my troubles, quirks, and insecurities back to me in cruel nursery rhymes. My belly has stuck to me through thick and thin. It is always close and warm. No matter how many times my parents moved our family to yet another state—from Pennsylvania to Michigan to Louisiana to Tennessee to New York, never staying longer than three years in any one place—my belly was a constant. It was my steady companion through years of being "the new girl," time and again. Whenever I sat alone at an otherwise empty table in a school cafeteria, agonizingly self-conscious and friendless, my belly snuggled right up against me and sat patiently in my lap. My belly had weight, too, even in its early days. It gave me the sense of having a cannonball-like core that made it harder for my short-tempered, bullying father to pick me up by the hair and drag me across the room. Maybe some part of me even imagined it made it more difficult to move me from one state to another.

People sometimes look at my belly and assume I'm pregnant. Total strangers approach me and press an overly familiar hand to my private abdomen and chirp, "Boy or girl?" I have a patent response for those people. I tip my head to the side, smile sweetly, and confess, "It's twin boys." I place a hand on one side of my protruding gut. "Ben"—then resting a palm on the other side of my belly—"...and Jerry."

Sometimes people look at my belly and assume I'm drowning in self-loathing. They assume I've given up on life. That I'm empty of goals and optimism. To them, I am the personification of slow suicide. And they imagine they see the evidence of my self-ruinous behavior around my middle.

The fact is, I adore life. I possess dreams and goals in abundance. I love to learn. I'm one of those people who gets aroused by a mailbox full of continuing-education catalogs every September. I want to learn every language, from Dutch to Lakota. I want to knit my own sweaters, repair my own car, and demonstrate Benihana-worthy knife skills in the kitchen. I want to know every Greek god and goddess by heart and be able to pick out little inaccuracies in any History Channel documentary, and to have *earned* the right to that pompous tsk-tsk as I shake my head and utter "Nice fact-checking there, History!"

I love to travel, too, and look forward to doing much more of it. I want to throw my head back and marvel at the pyramids of Egypt in person, feel the ancient sun like a white-hot mask upon my face. I want to skulk through the catacombs under Paris. I want to stay in an African hotel I saw on television where giraffes roam free on the property and poke their heads into the unscreened windows of the guest rooms. I want to write lots of books, perform many anonymous kindnesses, maybe even discover the true identity of Jack the Ripper.

My belly, and all my other fat, for that matter, was not amassed in an effort to destroy myself. On the contrary, my belly was built on a child's defiant will to *survive*.

Eating — *over*eating — saved me. It comforted me when I was at the mercy of grown-ups who didn't know how to give what I needed. Food was something to which I had ready access, and with it I cleverly fashioned a survival mechanism that pulled me back from the edge of insanity — a young MacGyver of angst and junk food. I, blessed with a genetic predisposition to anxiety, panic, and depression, managed to negotiate an insecure childhood and adolescence without ever landing in jail, becoming a junkie, getting knocked up, or hanging myself.

I don't overstuff my belly the way I used to. I reached a point where what I wanted *more* desperately than the twisted comforts of a bloated belly was freedom from its *discomforts*. I think finally becoming clear on why I'd been overstuffing myself for so many years helped me get there.

I get real hugs from people whose love is sincere. I don't need my belly to act as a half-assed mimic, simulating an embrace with its sickening pressure around my middle. My belly is no longer burdened with the additional responsibility of being my companion. I look to my fellow humans for healthy interaction. I don't face the same kinds of threats now that I did as a child, and I have methods at my disposal that help me feel grounded. I know better how to respond when threatened. I continue to work on finding grown-up ways to deal with life's challenges, actions that make sense and have a very real chance of leading to genuine solutions. The old habits are deeply ingrained and won't be easily waved off. But neither will I.

I stand turned forward, my belly preceding me. It is swollen. It is heavy. But as long as it belongs to me, I will move ahead anyway. I'll carry with me all that is mine until I don't need it anymore.

PART TWO

LOVING MY BODY

Curve: The loveliest distance between two points.

—Mae West

STRUT

One day while watching Turner Classic Movies, I heard a true story about Marilyn Monroe. She was strolling down a New York avenue with a friend, wearing an unremarkable dress with an ordinary scarf tied around her head. She went completely unnoticed.

Suddenly, the starlet turned to her companion and asked, "Would you like to see Marilyn now?"

It took her mere seconds to transform into a cinematic sex kitten. A subtle lifting of her shoulders, an alluring elongation of her back, the coy tilting of her head, and a suggestive swing of the hips, and *va-voom*! Immediately, people *noticed*. Our legendary bombshell was quickly surrounded by frantic admirers. She didn't have to duck into a phone booth and change into a sequined evening gown. And remember, her trademark platinum locks remained hidden under her head scarf. But this smart chickie knew how to create a full-blown scene with only the slightest adjustments in posture. No one on that Manhattan street cast an eye in Marilyn's direction until she made the conscious decision to strut her stuff.

Marilyn was able to transform herself from an ordinary woman into Marilyn Monroe just by adapting her walk and projecting the result she wanted onto people as she passed.

I was fascinated.

I was in my early twenties, living in my first apartment in an ugly brick building in a bustling, semi-suburban corner of Philadelphia, just a few blocks from my grandmother. The landlord was a cheap little man whose answer to insect complaints was to spray water around the outline of the kitchen sink with a plant mister and pretend he was exterminating. He had a dishwater white poodle that followed him around on maintenance visits, looking irreversibly miserable. The dog had a big, saggy pink growth on its left hind leg that looked like a human testicle.

I was making ends meet as best I could on a modest entry-level office worker's salary. I sorted mail and made photocopies for a corporate real estate firm in a high-rise building in Center City. I was estranged from my parents and had no secret benefactor — unless you count my friend Patrick, a fifty-something ex-hippie poet who'd left behind a high-paying job in corporate law to become a public defender. He was the gayest straight man I've ever known. Bald as a boiled egg. Goofy as all get-out. And yet something about his tiny glasses and ruddy cheeks and jowls put me in mind of an old founding father. He was a hairless Benjamin Franklin with a pot habit who waggled his eyebrows at anything provocative and added, "Woo-*woo*!"

Though Patrick was no secret, he was something of a benefactor, in that he occasionally fed me. We worked near each other and met for lunch once a week or so. He never let me pay for my own paper plate of pizza. Sometimes he even took me to dark, Frenchy little nooks where businessmen met with their mistresses, and we ate real food off white porcelain and made up stories about the illicit meals taking place all around us.

On weekends, I worked my second job in a tacky pan-
eled banquet hall for money under the table, setting plates
of chicken before the cheerless families of brides in polyester dresses. We were required to wear white tuxedo shirts
with black pants as a sort of uniform, and I remember being
so strapped for cash, I paid next to nothing for a display
shirt from the local tuxedo rental store that had the word
SAMPLE stamped across one of the lower front plackets. If I
kept a black apron tied high enough around my waist, you
wouldn't see the SA sticking out of my waistband.

My apartment was furnished with the bookcases I'd
brought from my bedroom in my parents' house and things
I found in the Sunday-night garbage. I slept on a sliver of
thick foam on the floor until my friend John cleaned out
his father's garage and found two 1950s camping cots.
"They're really disgusting, but they're better than nothing, so I thought you might want them." They had aluminum frames and criss-crossed wire stretched across them.
When you lay on one, your body sank to within an inch
of the floor. They came with skanky, moldy striped mat-
tresses, which my friend Parvin looked at with a lemon-
sucking face and obvious suspicion while saying, "Kimmy,
I don't think it's a good idea for you to sleep on those." I
zipped their skankiness inside a big vinyl mattress cover,
then duct-taped the frames together to create a queen-sized
frame. It wasn't comfortable, but it was mine. And besides,
when you walked into my bedroom, it finally *looked* like a
bedroom. There was something like a *bed* in it. A leopard-
print comforter from Woolworth's with a thread count of
twenty-two made it home.

I ate and drank what was cheap: hot dogs, noodles in
a cup, cans of generic vegetable soup, powdered iced tea
mix (watered down, made with half portions of powder
to make it stretch). Despite my humble means, I still man-

aged to gain back much of the weight I lost on ketosis. And I felt not only fat but shabby. I shopped at the Salvation Army and scoured the season-end sales at JCPenney. I covered stains with old brooches. I mended things. I colored over scuff marks on my shoes with black Magic Marker. I hoped no one would notice the fading or frayed edges, but they probably did.

I was carrying myself in a way that made me invisible. I was cultivating an opaque aura around me, because I decided I'd just rather go unnoticed.

When I heard the Marilyn story, it lodged inside my head and percolated there, until one day it occurred to me to conduct a little experiment.

It was lunchtime on a workday. I was walking south, crossing the major thoroughfares that cut through Center City, moving toward the narrower avenues lined with salad bars and pizzerias mobbed with hurried working stiffs. I was surrounded by others moving like a huffing tide in the same direction. Head down, eyes lowered, I could see their shoes, their calves. Occasionally, an old cobblestone poked defiantly through aging asphalt. My own shoes were getting soft and misshapen; a black thread was unraveling at the toe. And just then, I thought, *Do you want to see Marilyn now?*

Excitement tingled on my shoulders, like glitter falling from above.

I felt a charge simultaneously in my brain and at the base of my spine. I felt the corners of my eyes curling up a half second before my lips followed. I imagined I was confident, beautiful. I psyched myself into a state of absolute belief. I felt it in my body. I lifted my shoulders and immediately felt compelled to take a deep, cleansing breath. My limbs flooded with warmth and I felt my posture lifting and lengthening, felt my weight shifting from a burdensome sensation like a sandbag around my neck to a decisive, sure balance upon the backs of my hips. Then I let those hips sway. And there was something pleasurable about the way my weight shifted from one hip to the other, like dancing or swimming, or a pendulum with a satisfying density. I almost felt a little drunk.

As I approached a cross-street, the traffic signal turned red and I paused at the curb, feeling myself filling space with the full permission of the universe, oozing grace and sexuality. Then there was a voice from my right: "This is some gorgeous weather we're having, huh?"

I turned and faced the presence. He was an angelically handsome man with pale close-cropped hair, looking akin to Anderson Cooper or the Dyson vacuum cleaner man. He was impeccably dressed in a deep navy blue suit. Not dandy and accessorized enough to be gay, but just smart enough that he might be European or wealthy.

Holy crap! Men who looked like this *neeeeev*-ver started conversations with me! Especially not like *this*. Spontaneously. In public. Surrounded by other people who could easily snicker, and be heard snickering, for judging the man somehow faulty or perverse for chatting up a cow like me.

I smiled shyly and uttered some damp-rag response, like, "Yes, it is nice." Then I looked straight ahead. *Damn,* I hadn't counted on this working so *well*. I was struck dumb and didn't know where to take this. I had no small talk at the ready to keep the conversation rolling. I wasn't born to this sort of thing and had never taken a class in it. In retrospect I realize I could've called up the image of Glory Davis and channeled her easy way with men, but it didn't occur to me in the moment. A part of me was hoping he'd recognize how socially inept I was and take some pity, and be willing to do the work of drawing me out. But I don't think strangers bother to do that very often. To him it probably seemed I was sending a signal of disinterest.

When the traffic light turned, we both continued in the same direction, but I slowed my pace a little so he could move ahead. Then I paused and rested against the side of a building. I let Marilyn slip from my body like a silk robe to the ground, picked her up and folded her neatly away. I was left with a lump in my gut like some nasty, grassy farm turd and realized how much heavier my face felt when I was frowning. God, what an *idiot*! Even if I didn't want to date the man, maybe he could've been a friend. Maybe I would have grown somehow for knowing him. What was wrong with me?

I felt Marilyn's sharp elbow in my side. She was displeased with this train of thought.

I looked up the street and saw the top of a white-blond head bobbing along in the distance. Then I heard myself snort as I laughed. *Are we crazy, or did this stupid experiment actually* work?

There was definitely something to this. It was all in the way I carried myself. As if I felt like a million bucks. Hell, for those few moments I really *did* feel like a million bucks! And all that pulsating and emanating I imagined I was doing . . . well, I couldn't be sure, but it seemed at least one other person on that crowded sidewalk picked up on it. As if my radio signal was extrastrong and he'd tuned right in. And who knows what anyone else around me was thinking. And it had been easier than I thought. My god. I was a sorceress!

I'd observed the way women carried themselves when men turned to look at them. I always assumed all that breakneck gawking had to do with "perfect" bodies. But maybe it didn't. Not always. Or maybe a perfect body wasn't something that existed in the physical world, but was created in the imagination of the observer. And maybe the observer's vision could be influenced by the energy created by the person he's observing. Maybe when I believed I was powerful and perfect, others saw me that way. I'd projected the concept in my mind onto *their* minds, and when they observed me, it was like they were standing up close to a movie screen, seeing only what I, the projectionist, put there.

Maybe someone who sees "perfection" is responding not to what they think they're seeing, but to something else entirely. And maybe, I thought, that projection isn't always a conscious thing, like it was during my experiment. Maybe some people are so comfortable with themselves, so alive and free with who they are, that their movie projectors are always running on full power, and whoever stops in their tracks to watch that particular movie is responding from some place of deep truth within themselves. Maybe that's what falling in love is. We're recognizing what lights us up. And maybe that's how we find our soul mates and mentors and true friends.

And maybe people who let themselves get brainwashed by other people's prescriptions of beauty — like the legions of men buying in to the beer-commercial bikini ideal — aren't tuning in to the big radio station in the sky, in their hearts. They can't see the movie screen when it's playing to them and setting their faces aglow, because they're too busy squinting and focusing on the silhouettes of passersby along the base of the screen — people with their own separate paths to follow.

I was lying in my makeshift bed, splayed across the

uncomfortable bar in the middle where the two cots were taped together, staring through the semidarkness at an old Duran Duran poster I'd bought in the ninth grade. Its corners were crispy with layers of tape, applied, peeled up, and reapplied again and again as my family moved from one state to another. It was the only thing hanging on those otherwise blank eggshell white walls. I suddenly felt the urge to put on my Walkman and daydream. I wanted to visit with my fabulous alter ego, to cavort in her limitless universe for a while. But it was getting late and I had to get up for work in the morning. And I knew my downstairs neighbors would gripe at my footsteps crossing the creaky uncarpeted floor. I'd feel the pounding of a broom handle under my feet and the woman's voice shrieking, "Like a *horse,* I tell ya, she walks like a *horse!*"

So I stayed put.

But my mind churned.

Then I had a truly original thought.

All those positive reactions I imagined getting someday when I got thin — what if I could get them *while I was still fat*? What if I could be everything else I wanted to be — sexy, smart, successful — without ever having to be thin? What *if*?

It seemed to me that fat people were usually identified first by their fat. Everything else was secondary. You're always That Heavyset Girl in Accounting or The Fat Sister. And I knew I wasn't going to change overnight the way people think. But what if I had the power to scramble a few minds along the way? Wouldn't it be fun to play with a few heads? Guys' heads especially — cast my power of sexual projection upon them and leave them saying to themselves, "Jesus, that's the hottest fat girl I've ever seen." Leave them questioning themselves and their shallow beauty standards. Bewilder them with a fat girl's ability to give them a hard-on. Throw the world they thought they knew completely out of whack.

I began to suspect that when a woman fires up her own personal Marilyn, the first thing people see is that je ne sais quoi that shimmers around her and winks, "I'm special." Maybe her size gets shifted into second, or maybe even third or fourth place. Strutting. Who knew? It's psychological shapewear.

A picture of a new heroine started to form in my mind's eye. She looked a lot like me at my current weight, except she was fabulous. She was full-figured *and* captivating. She connected with the vehicle we call The Body, rather than dragging her person around like unwanted luggage. Everything below my neck had seemed so anonymous to me before, but this vision of who I could be, she claimed her body in full. She came to realize that her legs were her strongest body part. It pleased her to sense her calf muscles working for her. She put movement into her derriere. She walked with her chin up. She allowed her bosom to move as she breathed, let her rib cage rise and fall, took generous lungfuls without apology. And when she was seated, she struck an alluring posture. She allowed the mass of her body to rest comfortably and elegantly in a piece of furniture. She entered a room like she owned it, instead of retreating immediately to the darkest corner. She returned other people's gazes and smiles.

She was someone to be reckoned with. People wanted to be around her. They wanted to be her friend. She had her choice of sex partners and potential romances, if she wanted them. She could walk into any place — a restaurant, a shop, a company to apply for a job — and get exactly what she wanted. And everyone would forget that she was fat, because she was just so striking otherwise. Or, better yet, they'd see her fat and accept it as part of her striking whole, and acknowledge she'd be remarkable with *or* without it.

As I processed these novel thoughts, I also realized how often I didn't bother being pleasant toward other people, because I assumed they would dismiss me anyway, for being fat, or at least for my innate weirdness. Could I blame them for ignoring me? I walked around lead footed, with my chin to my chest in a twisted humanitarian effort to spare the world of my hideousness. I believed myself to be dumpy and ugly—and the populace was merely agreeing with me.

I dared myself to imagine radical self-acceptance, believing myself attractive and worthy of love and respect.

And I wouldn't have to fake it. Even as I continued to experiment with turning "Marilyn" on and off like a switch, I came to realize she wasn't someone I summoned from outside of me. She wasn't a character to be portrayed. She was the best part of me, insisting that her moment in the spotlight begin immediately and last as long as I live.

A TALE OF TWO PHOTO SESSIONS

"You know, Kim, you should've been up on that runway. You look better than all of those models did tonight."

It was Lou Greer, husband of my mother's friend Juanita. The Greers lived in our neighborhood, but my parents first met them at the Quartett Club, a social club where they were all members. I tended to steer clear of the Quartett Club, but was lured once to its clubhouse for a fashion show. It was there that jug-eared Lou Greer sauntered over and fondled me with his gaze. He was always looking at me hungrily. I wasn't flattered. I reasoned that at his age, anything under thirty looked good. I was a ripe, juicy seventeen. And Lou was obviously crazy. Models were thin. I was not.

My mother pointed out that there were so-called plus-size models.

"But it's not just the fat," I argued. "I have frizzy hair and a gap between my two front teeth. Models don't look like that. And am I even tall enough?"

"You're tall enough. Your teeth can be fixed, and you wouldn't have that problem with your hair if you rinsed the shampoo out correctly in the shower."

I rolled my eyes. The woman would never accept that my hair wasn't somehow my own fault.

"Look here in the Spiegel catalog," my mom said, flipping open her favorite monstrous mail-order catalog to the fat girls' section. She pointed to a brunette in a one-piece swimsuit, reclining backward against a rock. "All you'd have to do is work on your stomach. Look. See? Look at her legs. Look at her thighs, *they're* thick. This girl is heavy, but her *stomach* is completely flat. That's all you'd have to do. You wouldn't have to lose a lot of weight. Just do sit-ups and flatten your stomach."

Modeling was not my soul's calling, but there were things about the idea I liked. I liked that models got to wear funky clothes. I liked that they made lots of money, and lived in New York and Paris. And I liked that they were "somebodies." And besides, the idea of being a model—that is, a representation of ultimate beauty, after a lifetime of being fat and ugly—would mean some major validation.

So I entertained the thought. My mother took pictures of me in our sunroom with her 35-millimeter camera, a top-of-the-line Christmas present from Dad. We hung up solid bed sheets to create backdrops. I posed in different outfits. In some shots, we kept my hair naturally wavy. For others, my mother ironed my hair on the ironing board, so it would be shiny and straight. It was an old trick from the '60s. I'd kneel next to the ironing board and lean my scalp as close as possible into the padded surface. With the iron on a low setting, my mother pressed my hair stick straight. It was odd looking. Unnaturally straight, without any sort of flow, with an inch of wiry frizz from the scalp.

We took the pictures to a local modeling agency, and the lady said I'd need to lose about 20 pounds and that no one would see me without a portfolio of professional photos, both head shots and full body.

In the yellow pages, I found a photographer on Bainbridge Street who took portfolio photos for actors and models. His name was Alex Wenger. I took the train from my parents' far-flung suburban corner of Philadelphia into Center City, with a suitcase full of different styles of clothes, per Alex's instructions. I brought a 1960s bell-shaped black velvet jacket with black-and-white–striped satin lining; a 1920s white tuxedo with tails and black lapels; a black fedora; a purple satin blouse; a floral scarf.

Alex Wenger was a shaggy thirty-something guy with a spotty beard and longish, straight hair. He wore faded jeans that were baggy in the ass and an army green T-shirt. His studio was scattered with lamps and backdrops, stools and big wooden boxes painted black for posing on. The wall above his desk was covered in scraps of paper, magazine clippings and black-and-white photo prints, many of women's torsos with smallish breasts, their heads torn raggedly off. He offered me a glass of wine, but I refused. I'd sprung the extra fifty bucks for the makeup lady, who impressed me with her ability to resculpt my face with her variety of powders and creams. She thinned my nose, raised my cheekbones, and coaxed my deep-set eyes out of my face and made them sparkle.

"Oh wait, I brought something," I said to Alex, pulling a piece of paper from my pants pocket. "See how I have this giant gap between my two front teeth?"

He looked at my mouth, and I forced a toothy grin. He nodded.

"You sure do."

"Well, watch this. I know it's a weird idea but it actually makes a difference." I tore off a tiny strip of paper and plastered it behind my upper front teeth, pressing it into place with my tongue. My saliva created a temporary seal. "Thee?" I lisped. "It ack-tully redu-thess the appear-enths of the gap."

He arched his eyebrows and let his lower lip protrude. "You know what? You're right. That *is* weird. But it kinda works. Okay, so let's start."

We began with head shots. Some with my hair up, others with my hair falling over my shoulders. I changed tops several times, creating different moods. I feigned sophistication, devilishness, wistfulness.

Eventually we came to full-body shots. Alex led me across the room to a grouping of black-washed wooden boxes.

"Come on, you little sexpot, you," he said, then he belly-laughed, like he'd just made a damn good joke.

I didn't understand. I thought I was beautiful enough to be a model. Lou Greer thought so. Why was the idea that I was a sexpot so hilarious?

I followed his directions. I put on a pair of black corduroys, a black turtleneck, my big black velvet Carnaby Street jacket, the black fedora. I perched on the edge of a box, tilted my head into a false sun. He adjusted the lights so a black shadow fell purposely across my middle, right across my bump of a stomach. I felt awkward. I opted for pouting and melancholy, because I was finding it hard to smile.

When I got off the local commuter train near home, my mother and sister were there to meet me. Their faces shone with excited surprise when they saw me, still in my professional hair and makeup.

"Oh my god!" my mother yelped, grinning out of control. "You look like a totally different *person*!"

"Kim, you look so much older," my sister remarked.

"It's amazing what they can do with makeup," my mother added, scrutinizing my face up close and brushing back a curly lock of hair. "We should go out to dinner tonight so you can make the most of it. Show that face around in public before the makeup has to come off."

When we got home, I went straight up to the third floor of the house, where I had my bedroom and a little bathroom to myself. I closed the toilet seat and sat on it, regarding myself in the mirrored medicine cabinet opposite.

What's pretty? I wondered. What *is* beautiful? *You should've been up on that runway.* Sarcasm: *Come on, you little sexpot, you.* A laughingstock. A collection of facial features maturing into a bland, forgettable visage. Maybe I had a face like one of those quirky visual puzzles they sometimes publish in newspapers or comic books. It looks like nothingness, a mess of lines or pixels until you stare at it long enough. Then you see an old woman upside down, or Abraham Lincoln. Some people never see it. Maybe if you have kaleidoscope eyes, like an insect, you see something beautiful when you look at me. It's a trick. And maybe it only works with men over fifty, whose eyes are starting to go. Hip people, young people, creative men with artists' eyes, trained to really "see" beauty, like photographers, saw a joke of a girl. A belly to be blotted out in shadow. Thick, cellulite-ridden thighs like pockmarked ham hocks. Someone to overlook in favor of childlike torsos with champagne-glass breasts. The way I saw it, fat canceled out any trace of prettiness that flickered across a girl's face, any potential for love-at-first-sight.

I never had been right, deep down. And I would never be beautiful. Only my grandmother knew how to love me. My dear little grandmother with her beaklike nose and tiny eyes, her father's favorite. He'd always called her his "ugly duckling."

"I hate you," I said matter-of-factly to the painted face in the mirror. My jaw stiffened. "I hate you!" I screamed. "I *hate* you!" I picked up the nearest thing—a bottle of shampoo on the edge of the bathtub. I hurled it at my reflection with all my strength. The medicine cabinet bounced open, but the mirror didn't shatter. The bottle cap flew off and spread golden syrupy shampoo across the checkered floor in a wide teardrop puddle. I regarded it almost calmly.

"I hate you," I whispered again, then stepped over the shampoo mess to the sink and began to scrub my face clean.

A week later I returned to Alex's studio to collect the negatives and several contact sheets. The contact sheets showed the strips of photo negatives printed as rows of tiny developed images.

He sat at his desk, hunched over the sheets, studying the shots through a loupe. With a wax pencil he circled the ones he recommended I have printed for my portfolio. As his eyes perused the images, he said with a concentrated frown, "You know, you kinda have a cool face."

Then he shrugged and shuffled the sheets and negatives into a neat pile, pushed them into a manila envelope, and handed it to me. We were done here.

"Oh, my God." My mother slapped the steering wheel in percussive disbelief. "Can you believe the *nerve* of that woman? Where does she get off wearing a skirt that short? At her size, she's got no business!"

We were driving along Byberry Road, past the old abandoned lunatic asylum. A fat woman was walking with relaxed purpose along the side of the road in a black miniskirt and T-shirt. Her arms and legs were thick and alabaster, her rear end ample and heart shaped.

It was summer and I was fat, too. I wore jeans and a boatneck tunic with three-quarter-length sleeves to hide my sausagelike upper arms and flabby elbows. I was keeping my fat to myself, sparing the public of my hideousness. Just as "The Elephant Man" John Merrick wore a burlap sack over his head when walking the streets of London. It was a simple matter of courtesy.

I was in my twenties then. By my late thirties, I was still wearing three-quarter-length sleeves in summer, and I'd only bare my legs when I swam. But the difference was, I no longer thought my body was ugly. I'd arrived at a place where I thought my body was beautiful. I still do.

To the touch, I'm scrumptious. The pinkish white swells of my hips, breasts, and belly beg to be caressed, stroked — *kneaded* like so much pie dough. And if you've ever actually kneaded dough, or pressed your fingers into a lump of dense but pliable clay and felt the sweet, aching satisfaction in your hands as you molded it — feeling it give beneath your palms, subtly varying the pressure from your fingertips as you slid them across the endlessly fascinating surface — then you know the pleasure of a body like mine beneath your touch.

Aesthetically, I'm pear-shaped. The contrast between my waist and hips is dramatic and unmistakable. It's an exaggeration of femininity, like a promise of extreme fertility.

For an observer to be aroused by the sight of me should not be surprising, because my fat casts a floodlight on my pelvic area and is shamelessly suggestive not only of the babies to which I was designed to give passage but also of the sexual stimulation of which I am capable. It is a pelvis that can writhe with abandon and thump like a bass drum in arousal. The sway of my generous hips is like a neon yellow highlighter wiped over the word *woman*. My oversized hips are a bullhorn screaming, "Woman!" I am a siren song to every other human being capable of seeping with desire for the female form. I am woman — *lots* of woman, abundant woman, *ultimate* woman.

This is what breast implants are meant to do, you know. Cast a magnifying glass over the inherent womanliness of breasts and *attract*. Women get boob jobs to give themselves a certain edge. Frankly, I don't see why they nearly kill themselves trying to diet off their equally bulbous hips. Besides, my belly feels just like a nippleless breast. It's like one giant porn boob implanted at my waist — a sexual bonus, if you will.

Archaeological discoveries like the Venus of Willendorf have taught us that early peoples, untainted by contemporary definitions of the body "ideal," really responded to the big-hipped, big-bellied woman. They idolized her, literally. And when I see myself naked, I see that body worthy of worship.

Everything changed when I got my first digital camera. It was a gift, and it came with a tripod. Alone in my apartment one afternoon, I decided to look at myself — *see* myself as I actually was. I pulled the blinds and stripped down to my cheap polyester bra and teal cotton granny-panties. I slipped on my black satin special-occasion pumps, then erected the tripod at the end of the hallway that led from the front door. Pressing the camera button for a ten-second delay, I hustled to the opposite end of the hall and stood, hands-on-hips, letting the camera's flash shower me in white. I returned to the camera and reached for it, tentatively. I looked in the viewer.

Yep. I was fat. And at the same time, something about

my body pleased me—the milky fullness, the inviting to-pography of its curves. So I set the timer again, this time to take my picture as I sashayed *away* from the camera, capturing me in movement.

I was stunned by how sexy I looked. I'm talking drop-dead *bombshell* sexy. The kind of sexy that makes sailors in movie musicals spin 180 degrees on their heels and whistle, white hats comically askew or twisted in their hands.

There was a line to my body like an elongated *S* that riveted me. And I liked the way one of my ass cheeks cocked upward as I threw my leg forward. Like a wry smile, or the cheerful buttocks in the old Underalls commercial that made a cute staccato xylophone sound with each side-to-side wag.

I liked these pictures. I liked the body in them.

Now I understand why every lover I ever had couldn't resist tucking their hands into the warm, baby-smooth pockets of skin on either side of my pudendum, just under the fold of my overhanging belly. I understand the pas-sionate abandon with which one man took my left leg into both arms as he knelt before my reclining body and kissed the leg's thickness, stroked it wildly from tree-trunk calf to thunder-thigh, his eyelids half lowered in a state of near-madness, overcome, a stream of pleasing filth drip-ping from his slack lips. I no longer discount the lovers who reveled in the rolling cashmere expanse of my ass as having had "something wrong" with them.

Do people view fat women as unsexy because it's what they've been taught since birth? And are they eating that opinion obediently off a spoon like a dozy infant in a high chair?

We look at fat women and are conditioned to think their thick limbs and juicy middles are putrid. But these same features fail to disgust us in other contexts.

We bite into a plump and succulent fruit with relish.

We put the corpulent plaster bodies of cherubs on display in our gardens, on our bedspreads in one-dimensional brushed cotton, and on glossy paper we frame and hang in our powder rooms.

Every fleshy newborn baby inspires cooing and cuddling. We can't resist fondling their soft, stout, and unshapely limbs, tickling their pudgy bellies and nuzzling their swollen apple cheeks.

Every time I see a dog show on TV, I'm struck by how fervently we adore our fat little breeds of dogs: the endearing rotundity of lumbering bulldogs and chubby pugs, the sad heavy-lidded eyes and loose sagging skin of the sweet shar-pei. We derive joy from the appearance of these creatures. We can't resist reaching out for them, encircling their barrel bodies with affectionate hands.

We survey lush landscapes with variations not dissimilar to an "imperfect" female body with absolute pleasure—say, an expanse of Irish countryside with grassy rolling hills, and clusters of boulders and sudden valleys, gullies and ridges and bald patches. Do these wide swaths of earth nauseate us? Is it really so much uglier when it's made of flesh instead of soil?

I think men in particular are ashamed to admit to their buddies, even to their families, when they find themselves attracted to a fat woman. Sometimes I think they sublimate their natural desires just to keep up appearances. And that's just plain unhealthy.

When I lived in New York City, I eventually stopped riding the subway because I was tired of being molested. Every other trip it seemed I was getting grabbed or squeezed or jizzed on. I've seen some clever, applause-worthy ruses for trying to get a hand on a boob. I even sent a stalker to jail—a wiry, drunken fool whom I first

noticed when he tried to slip his hand under my ass while
I sat. Men did stripteases to impress me; they pulled it out
and shamelessly started whacking off as they stared.

Men were literally taking their desires *underground*.

That's not to say I haven't been hit on aboveground,
too. The male model from Israel who practically broke his
neck to get a good look at me in the nightclub—*and* get
my number. The native Italian taxi driver who breath-
ily confessed that he couldn't keep his eyes off of me in
the rearview mirror. As I dozed upright in the back seat,
he'd wished he could kiss me—"You a-looked a-like
an *angel*!"

Not that long ago, I was ashamed of myself. Ashamed
that I wasn't strong enough to be the woman in that private living room photo shoot every day. It took some time.
It used to be, when skin was bared to the emerging sun
of summer, eagerly unwrapped and unsweatered and
flaunted in the light of day, what kept me covered up was
the disgust I imagined other people feeling for my body. I
didn't want to tempt cruel comments, didn't want to imagine the ones people might be making as they drove by.

I didn't want anyone to think less of me because of how
I looked. I didn't want people to miss my engaging personality, my wealth of good jokes and even better ideas, just
because they were distracted by the details of my fatness:
the translucent tiger stripes of my stretch marks; cellulite
like a dappling of fairy fingerprints on my skin. I wanted
a fair chance. For a job and equal pay, for a table near the
front of the restaurant, for courtesy when I shopped in a
high-end store, for lasting friendship, for unconditional
love, for everyday kindness. So I hid my fat as best I could.

I didn't just wake up one morning and find myself in a
state of complete and radical self-acceptance. It was a gradual process, like easing oneself into a pool of cold water,

one inch at a time, or gingerly and systematically removing a mediocre painted landscape from a canvas to reveal an earlier, priceless masterpiece underneath. I was gentle with myself. I emerged from my cocoon in patient time. All the while, I was growing stronger in there. So strong that when I finally spread my wings and bared my arms, nothing anyone might say about them could possibly hurt me.

MY GRANDMOTHER: FOREVER IN MY ARMS

Something significant happened in the days before my grandmother passed, when I spent a lot of time thinking about her, trying to solidify her physicality (among other things) in my memory, knowing I would never see her again. Of all the epiphanies I could've experienced during my grandmother's death, the last thing I expected was a new perspective on my self-image.

When I was small, my grandmother was a chubby woman. She lost weight later in life and became a tiny, featherweight sprite of an old lady. But when I remember cuddling with her as a preschooler, I clearly remember her big belly. Sometimes I liked to lay my head in her lap, and her belly made a wonderful pillow. Beneath her thin cotton housedresses that always smelled of Ivory soap, her middle was lumpy and soft, yet supportive. It was a comforting middle I'd thrown my arms around countless times as she stood at the stove heating alphabet soup in a saucepan for my lunch, or when she hugged me on my way out the door to return to my mother.

My grandmother's later, slimmer figure betrayed clues of her once-higher weight—like on her upper arms where the skin hung loose in fleshy flaps. But that loose skin was also the softest skin you could imagine, as soft as a newborn baby's. Often I'd stroke her flabby arms and say, "Mmmm, your skin feels like dewy rose petals," and she'd laugh or tell me I was "crazy, kid" or make a disparaging remark about her "ugly" upper arms.

In the most brutally honest core of my being, I cannot agree that my grandmother's flabby arms were ugly, or for that matter, anything less than lovely. They were my grandmother's arms, and they smelled clean and sweet and felt divine. I loved them, because they were a part of her.

I always had a special bond with my grandmother. We were close, but not in that secret-sharing, uncounted-hours-of-meaningful-conversation kind of way. She was a much simpler person than I am. Simpler and more reticent.

My grandmother liked to watch *Lawrence Welk* and listen to sermons on AM radio. She disliked disruption, wore pale blue and lavender, and read the same Christian romance novels over and over again. Each time she finished one, she'd write her name and the date she completed it inside the front cover. Her world was small and quiet and routine, and I think it made her feel safe.

Before my father moved our family away from my grandmother when I was five, I spent a lot of time with her. I never wanted to leave her side. I wanted to be in whatever room she was in. Even without her hugs and kisses I would've sensed her tender regard on an intuitive level. As a child, being with her made me completely and utterly happy in a way nothing and no one else did. On the sofa, I curled up at her side and caressed her baby-fine silver hair, plastered her face with kisses, and cupped my small, rosy hands around her own knotty, speckled, velveteen-soft hands. When I told her I loved her, she always said, "I love you too, kiddo."

As I got older, oblivious to how I might be expected to

curtail my childlike interactions with my grandmother (or maybe just not giving a damn), I always fell quite naturally and comfortably into our long-established routine. "I want to sit next to *you,* Grandmom," I insisted — and at age four, twelve, nineteen, twenty-four, thirty, I snuggled up at her side and took her hand in mine.

In the presence of my grandmother, I returned to a place most of us leave behind for good in early childhood, a place where we feel and speak our truth without self-censoring or self-consciousness. A place from which we look upon bodies — both our own and the bodies of others — with curiosity, incapable of cruel scrutiny. We notice that some people are taller than others, that some people have skin that's a darker or lighter shade than our own. And some bodies are larger and thicker than others. I think of my friend Kathleen's daughter, whom I adore, who climbs into my lap without hesitation and grabs my face between her miniature palms, presses her nose to mine, and says, "I love you, Kimmy"; and who innocently observed and announced without judgment, "Kimmy, you have a big butt."

There was a time when I couldn't imagine anything more frightening than my beloved grandmother dying. I remember being thoroughly convinced that her inevitable death would mark the end of my sanity; that I simply wouldn't be able to handle the concept of this woman no longer existing in the same world with me. It was difficult to imagine her not being out there *somewhere,* sitting in front of the television, watching *The Price is Right* and awaiting a visit from one of her doting children or grandchildren.

Her eventual dementia — which most of her seven children patently refused to call Alzheimer's, as if that somehow made the situation less dire, less permanent — was an effective buffer between my fear of losing my grandmother and her inevitable demise. It helped me ease into the good-bye. The disease made her unrecognizable from behind those wide, glassy eyes, so that in a sense, she was gone long before she actually died. Once her mind was gone, so was the woman I knew as my grandmother. The woman who walked hardily to and from the Salvation Army church every Sunday in thick-heeled shoes, even when she was well into her eighties. The woman who'd scold me in adulthood for slipping up and saying "Oh my God" (it was taking the Lord's name in vain). The same woman who sent me into a laughing fit when I asked her what she thought of my aunt's new husband and she turned to me with a curled upper lip and said, "He's a *nerd*."

Her dementia gave me time to get used to having lost her, though for a while I still had her warm skin to ca-ress, and her familiar, comforting body to embrace. When I held her, I tried to transmit soothing love into her body via sheer will, though I knew she would never be herself again. The Alzheimer's gave her the expression of a con-tented infant. It made her speak like a child.

"Russell," she'd say to my uncle, who'd been her live-in caretaker since before I was born, "when are we going home?"

"You *are* home, Ma," he'd tell her gently, every time as though she was asking for the first time. One day she looked up as I walked into her living room and asked, "Are you my daughter?" I knelt by her chair and stroked her face tenderly with my hand. "No, I'm your granddaughter. And I *looooove* you." I kissed her forehead and she smiled and giggled like a little girl.

"Do we love each other?" she asked.

"Mm-hm," I nodded. She gestured to my uncle with an arthritic finger.

"And do you love him, too?"

"Yep," I said. "He's my uncle Russell."

Her eyes traveled between my uncle and me and she proclaimed, "Then we all love each other, don't we? We all love each other here!"

I couldn't help letting out a small laugh. In spite of everything, she was awfully cute.

Although my grandmother was much shorter than I, as I get older I can see the similarities between her heavier figure and mine. When I catch a glimpse of my own thick calves in a mirror, I flash back to seeing Grandmom's legs peeking out from under a gingham snap-on dress as she crossed the living room and stood at the window, overlooking Rising Sun Avenue with her hands on her hips.

I have my grandmother's former belly, and in truth, at moments when I collapse backward into my plump, inviting sofa and lose myself in the TV, I like to pull my belly out of my pants and rest my hands on it. It's warm and soft and comforting. I'm done hating it. Hating the fact that it's too big to even get sucked in anymore, hating the way it makes me look pregnant in sweatshirts and sweaters.

How can I hate something on my own body that I was capable of *adoring* on my grandmother's? My grandmother was lovable exactly the way she was. I say this with the greatest authority. Not even loved *in spite of* her physical "imperfections," but *because* of them. So why should it be so difficult to love my own body, regardless of what stage it's in? Why indulge in the preposterous idea that I am unlovable because my stomach, my arms, my ass, my thighs, are not what a shallow money-driven media tells me they should be? My grandmother could not have been more cherished — not just by me, but by her other grand-

children, her own children, her siblings, and the legion
of friends she left behind at her beloved Salvation Army
church.

If I do lose my belly, or any other mounds of fat, I'll be
left with lots of loose skin where my chub once was. There
are plenty of doctors out there who've perfected the art of
trimming post-weight loss skin, and I must admit, in the
past I was willing to consider the idea. But trimming my
arm skin is no longer an option. It would break my heart
to get rid of something that reminds me so much of my
dear grandmother—the only warm, living-flesh representation I have of her.

My grandmother existed in a tiny world outside of popular culture and its poisonous prescriptions, a world with
many tiny worlds within it. One of them was the little
universe where her heart and mine coexisted. There were
no thoughts of supermodels or sucking it in between us.
There was only her and me, and the incomparable bliss we
felt when we sat together, hand in hand, enjoying being
together. And that love and sense of absolute belonging
was bigger than any worry I've ever had about how I
looked in a sleeveless dress. It was bigger than my belly
at its biggest, or the biggest-size jeans I've ever bought to
accommodate it. It was—it *still* is—bigger than any big
jerk who has something petty and critical to say about the
shape of a woman's body, mine or anyone else's.

I have decided to honor my body—flabby arms
and all—for myself, and for the enduring love of my
grandmother.

GYM DANDIES

I'll never be one of those sleek, adrenaline-pumped people in a commercial for high-tech sneakers or sports drinks, grimacing in steely determination with a toe poised on the edge of a starting line, grabbing life by the humid balls one steep mountain-bike path at a time, sweating electro-lyte blue droplets with glorious abandon.

Impossible. Because I hate exercise.

To me, exercise is a big, bullying bruiser who's all too happy to push me to the brink of death. It is a doomful march at gunpoint through a syrup-aired tropical jungle. It's being face up on a gurney, unable to tell the huddle of white coats around me what hurts, so they cannot help me.

And I hate that I feel this way. It seems unnatural.

You would think, as part of a built-in mechanism to promote survival of the human species, that we would *all* have an innate desire to jump and run and flail our limbs around on a chalk-lined field.

So why is it that some of us *don't*?

As a kid, playing outdoors with other kids was never an alluring prospect. Especially when it involved a ball or moving my body rapidly from one place to another.

It just seemed I was born for more sedentary pursuits.

I wanted to be left alone, with Newbery Award—winning books and college-ruled spiral notebooks, freshly sharpened pencils and my favorite felt-tip purple pens. For sure, I had the cerebral thing taken care of—but why didn't I feel a more natural pull toward the physical?

Maybe it was the frightening state that exercise put my body in, so reliably, every time.

Running even the shortest distance made my heart pound so loudly in my head, it partially deafened me to everything outside. And it beat far too fast for any activity that was meant to be fun. A voice throbbed in my ears, *This* can't *be healthy! I'm going to have a heart attack!*

The accompanying shortness of breath was terrifying. I'd look around at all these kids frolicking and having fun and think, *They can't* possibly *be experiencing what I am right now, or they'd be sprawled on the grass* dying!

Clearly *their* lungs, unlike mine, had not shut down, collapsed into themselves like two popped gum bubbles, two pink layers clinging together, no open space to fill, just me and a dead-end sort of choking. I strongly suspect I had childhood asthma that went undiagnosed.

So no, exercise did not equate to joy in my life. It meant extreme discomfort and the fear of death.

If you went to public school in the United States, no doubt you remember the Presidential Physical Fitness Test—a battery of events meant to test your strength and stamina, the mastery of which earned you a navy blue embroidered patch at an end-of-school-year ceremony.

In the sixth grade, my best friend, Simone Shanker, and I were kind of famous for being bad at the Presidential Physical Fitness Test. We were the only two kids in the entire grade who never, ever passed a single Fitness Test event—that is, never met the minimum requirements to be deemed "fit." We couldn't even pass the "easy" ones,

like the long jump. The long jump required you to bend
your knees, swing your arms energetically at your sides,
then launch yourself forward, sneakers together. No matter
how emphatically I tried, I could never jump far enough.

It seemed like the popular girls with the nicest clothes
always passed the Fitness Test without trying very hard.
They always got the stupid blue patch. They could do the
most sit-ups in a row without stopping. They could cross
the monkey bars hanging from their toothpick arms as easily as they walked from one end of the mall to the other.
They could run the 600-yard walk/run without choking
for breath.

I never quite understood the correlation between peer
acceptability and athletic prowess. Maybe it's something
written deeply on our genetic material. Survival of the fit-
test, literally speaking. Simone and I were destined to be
the last of our flabby, bookish kind. (Although now that
people aren't chased down by wild boars as routinely as
we once were, I wonder if the idea of ultimate, enviable
"fitness" could stand some retooling to include equal parts
of athletic *and* intellectual agility?)

Simone and I reliably brought up the rear on the 600.
A 600-yard run seemed an impossible feat to me and I got
nervous about it weeks before it happened. We had to run
around the entire school building *three times*! Simone and I
slouched our way around a lazy second lap and skipped the
third lap altogether. There wasn't enough time in an entire
gym period for Simone and I to make it three times around.

The message was clear: I just wasn't cut out for sporty
things. There was something wrong with me. I was abnor-
mal. Un*fit* for society. And the whole Fitness Test horror
was further proof that I was unacceptably *fat*.

But I had additional reasons for avoiding all things athletic. Like not wanting to get hit in the face with a ball.

As an adult, I'm comforted to know I'm not alone in this. Recent conversations with friends have revealed there were like-minded kids all over the country who valued their noses and teeth.

With us, this ball phobia ripened with age into a piquant blend of belligerence and proud disinterest in team sports. Our classmates hated us for it, of course. My friend Kathy zealously confessed that during gym games, the ball would come to her and she'd cross her arms to make *sure* she didn't catch it—complete with a kiss-my-ass smile.

I remember being forced to play softball in gym, but having no idea what was going on, nor did I care to learn. Always last to be chosen for a team, I'd be cast off into the outfield, where I daydreamed I was in a Minnesota flower field in a calico dress, Laura Ingalls Wilder's unwritten chubby sister, just a stone's throw from our darling little house on the prairie. Unaware of the sporting machinations going on around me, I pondered how they got Tootie to look so much older for her short stint as a supermodel on *The Facts of Life,* and decided with some irritation that Mrs. Garrett was being overly protective—so what if a twelve-year-old girl snarled into the camera? And no doubt I was thinking, *This sun is so hot! And there are gnats in this grass!*

And yes, the occasional ball would bounce past me on the dewy lawn, and suddenly everyone would be yelling at me. Oh, wait—was I supposed to *catch* that?

Oddly enough, I'm reminded here of Ralphie in that classic holiday movie *A Christmas Story,* when he's waiting in line to see Santa Claus, and the Wicked Witch of the West cheerfully accosts him. "Don't bother me," he says to her dismissively, "I'm . . . I'm thinking."

That's me today, faced with a world of gym memberships and upwardly mobile Rollerblading couples and impromptu volleyball games between neighbors. Don't bother me with that painful, sweaty stuff—I'm *thinking*. It's who I think I am. A thinker, not a mover. It's what I've come to believe.

But I understand that bodies *need* activity to stay healthy, energetic, and mobile. Herein lies the problem. How can I learn to love something I hate, in order to have the happiest, longest life possible?

My attempts at engaging in regular exercise have been spotty. I remember in my late teens, the one big motivator that led me to hire a driving teacher and get my license was the ability to go to the gym at any time, day or night. For once in my life, I was going to get it right. I was going to be like the healthy, pretty people in the big plate-glass windows at Bally's, all rosy cheeked with their moist brows and firm upper arms, pumping away at their daily workouts like machines, with the same happy mindlessness of toothbrushing. Like them, I was stepping up and choosing vitality.

The truth is, I used the car to drive to the gym only once. After that it became the daily bus to Taco Bell, departing at three p.m. for snacks from the drive-through.

For a while in my late twenties, I was successful at committing to regular walking. I talked my then-boyfriend into buying a motorized treadmill that folded up against the wall of our tiny Manhattan apartment. It worked because I replaced my lifelong habit of pacing around with my Walkman on while daydreaming, with daydreaming on the treadmill instead. I got so lost in the music and my imagination that I'd end up walking uphill for forty-five minutes before I even noticed I was exercising. But one too many times, I landed with a foot off the treadmill belt and tripped, being yanked into the present in a way that was both mentally and physically jarring. Like George Jetson,

I stumbled and groped for something to hold as the belt tried to flick me off the back of the treadmill like a swollen mosquito off a forearm. After that, I realized I wasn't achieving the same depth of mental escape anymore. I had to keep my thoughts at least partially on the placement of my feet. It kept me frustratingly too close to the surface of my mind, too conscious. Being aware of the work my body was doing made me exhausted and bored. I abandoned the machine.

Several years ago, on the advice of my former therapist, I agreed to a free trial session with her personal trainer. She recommended him highly, said he wasn't like other trainers: "He's very patient and insightful...very *Zen*." Being that she knew me well and specialized in helping large-size women with eating disorders, I trusted her judgment.

This bald and beefy little black man in linen with a collection of Buddha figurines, who'd left behind Wall Street to bring people into better balance with their bodies, completely sucked *ass*.

He pushed me beyond my limits. He pushed and he pushed.

I told him as soon as I walked in the door, "Look, dude, here's the thing. I hate exercise. And the only way this is going to work is if I feel I have a chance in hell of doing this long-term. I have to *want* to come back." I thought I made it clear that I didn't want the workout to be too hard at first, that I needed to work my way up *slowly*. Much more slowly than most people. If I left panting and exhausted and deafened by my own heartbeat, chances were, he'd never see me again. In that state, I'd gladly sign up for ten to twenty years of my life if it meant I didn't have to go through *that* torture again. He nodded sagely and I thought he understood me.

Halfway through the session I stopped and looked at him incredulously. I was red faced and a salty waterfall cascaded from my scalp. "Did you not hear what I said? This is *too much*!"

"Well, I have to make you do a certain minimum, you know?" He sounded exasperated. "If I don't do that, then I'm not doing my job. I can't let you leave here knowing I didn't at least give you the minimum I know you need to see a difference."

I'm sorry, but you won't convince me that doing only twenty lifts on each arm instead of forty would've done me *no* good whatsoever. Because you see, at twenty reps, I might've felt like, "Hey! I can do this!" Yes, *encouraged*. I might've come back to him, determined to do twenty-five, thirty, forty, or more.

But instead, I left frustrated, feeling like the poster child for Athletic Imbecility. It was sixth-grade gym class all over again. A minimum had been set, and if I couldn't meet it with a smile on my face, then I was a physical reject.

Furthermore, did you catch that last thing he said? The "minimum I know you need to *see a difference*"? In hindsight, I realized this dumbbell was completely appearance focused. For him, my success (and his) was defined by how my body *looked*. Nothing I'd said about wanting more energy, stamina, and overall strength had really sunk in. For him, this was about reshaping a lumpy fat girl. All those other benefits fell into a fringe category.

Like so many personal trainers, I don't think he believed physical fitness *could* be achieved until a body not only *looked* a certain way but also weighed a certain weight. The misconception that only a body that's sleek and slim and muscular — classically "athletic" — can possibly be "fit" discourages many people from getting active. They see fitness as an intimidating uphill climb, a body ideal that would take a lifetime of fanatical attention to attain, if it was even genetically possible for them at all.

This is indeed sad, because one doesn't have to achieve a certain prescribed body weight or appearance to *be* fit. And there are plenty of living examples out there, athletes who in everyday life might be looked upon as "fat slobs" who are powerhouses on the softball field, in the gym, on the track, in the pool, on their bikes.

Doesn't make sense to you? Think about it. Imagine a woman who's five-foot-seven and weighs 200 pounds. She's got thick thighs, thick upper arms, and a bit of a belly. Her cholesterol, blood pressure, and blood sugar are stellar. You *wish* you had her lab workup. And she's a tri-athlete. And she's the star of her regional softball team.

According to the height and weight chart issued by the popular local weight loss center, she should lose about 70 pounds.

She could walk into the office of a physician she's never seen before, and he might take one look at her figure and say, "First things first—you need to lose some weight."

You might look at her standing in line at the post office and think, *God, I hope I never look like her. I want to be* healthy.

What more does this woman have to do? And *why*?

When all the health excuses are shot to hell, you're left with a longing to be attractive, and to make your friends wish they were hot like you. Let's at least be honest about it and stop pretending so many of these extreme workouts are for the sake of longevity.

I hope Mr. Zen Trainer has become more enlightened since I last saw him.

I wrote and appeared in a video for people who, like

me, hate exercise (and/or have physical limitations), encouraging them to find exercise they enjoy — exercise that feels more like play than work. I also urged viewers to feel comfortable taking baby steps toward getting more active.

In response, I received a patronizing e-mail from a woman who's both a marathoner and a fitness blogger. She told me my advice was irresponsible because "you need to do at least thirty minutes of exercise five days a week in order to get any physical benefit."

What is it with these fitness preachers who insist that no exercise is good exercise unless it's at least "this much"? So many of them claim to be advocates for improved health. They claim to be in the *service* of out-of-shape people. If any of this were true, they would understand that many people cannot do "this much," and may not be able to do "this much" for quite some time — perhaps never. If a person tries to do too much on day one, he or she may never show up for day two. How is putting a person in that position in any way a genuine effort to get him or her on the road to improved fitness?

And don't try to tell me that even ten minutes of light walking once a week won't give *any* benefit to someone who's otherwise completely sedentary. At the very least, it may have mood-elevating effects and help prevent vascular issues caused by sitting too long.

By suggesting that anything less than "this much" exercise is a waste of time, trainers are being uncaring, unprofessional, and dismissive. Without saying it explicitly, they're still telling us that anyone not fit enough to do "this much" right off the bat is not worth helping at all. It's like they're advocating letting the "unfit" die off until no one but a superfit Master Race remains.

There's yet another breed of fitness buffs who do more

to hurt flabby people than help them: people whose grand passion is fitness, and like anyone with a grand passion, they can't wait to share it with anyone willing to listen.

Passion is a wonderful thing, but some of these fitness enthusiasts have tunnel vision. They can't conceive of anyone not wanting to devote their lives to physical fitness with the same fervor *they* do. Some of them even feel superior and self-righteous about it. They take every opportunity to insinuate that people who don't prioritize exercise are morally inferior, like sticky scraps of garbage clinging to the edges of society, a costly burden to the *truly* fit of the world. We're an embarrassing mess to be either cleaned up or shipped off on barges to the far reaches of the planet where we can be neither seen nor smelled.

If you pay close enough attention, you'll find this message *everywhere*—in ad copy, quipped on sitcoms. The message is delivered in the slickest of ways, designed to make you feel simultaneously ashamed of yourself and pumped up to join the fitness-is-next-to-godliness movement. Like when a television fitness guru points a chastening finger at you through your plasma screen and barks, "NO EXCUSES!"

Really? Are there truly *no* excuses for failing to put exercise first above *all else*?

We live in an age of two working parents and single parents who must work multiple jobs. So, after earning a living, preparing dinner, and possibly even preparing lunches for an entire family for the next day, if a parent chooses to spend the couple of hours he or she has left helping a child with homework or simply connecting with that child, is that choice really so worthy of the snot-nose bullying of our culture's self-important fitness icons? Raising *decent human beings,* regardless of whether or not they

look like the "after" pictures in a Xenadrine commercial is
a worthwhile pursuit.

I'm not saying that people *shouldn't* make an effort to
incorporate more physical activity into their busy lives.
We've all read the magazine tips. Take the stairs instead!
Park on the far end of the parking lot and walk the rest
of the way! Create quality time by going on a family bike
ride instead of sitting in front of the tube! There's nothing wrong with these suggestions, if you also take into account the realistic circumstances of most Americans today.
Many of these helpful "tips" may not get executed five to
seven days a week, fifty-two weeks a year. And if they
don't, that doesn't make us bad people.

And while it makes sense to seek advice from an expert
on a given subject—for example, to consult with someone obsessed with plumbing to learn how best to fix our
pipes—maybe in some cases, we should be smart enough
to see when an obsession has gone a little too far, to incorporate the advice in moderate ways that make sense for
us and leave the rest. (You get the best pipes you can afford within your budget—even when the plumbing en-
thusiast tells you, "And then there's *copper*...the *only*
pipe I use.")

Maybe that's what America needs to do as it watches
The Biggest Loser by the millions, and considers the "be-
nevolent" advice of its fitness-obsessed TV trainers. We're
led to believe their preoccupation with exercise is superior
because of its connection to good health, when the desire
to be healthy is seen as such a virtue.

I don't know about you, but I wouldn't trust my body
to anyone who puts out-of-shape people through such extreme physical training. There's a lot to be said for mod-
eration in exercise. There's less risk of injury, and the

exerciser is more likely to stick with activity they build upon gradually.

Besides, *The Biggest Loser* takes a warlike approach to transforming its contestants, and it rubs me the wrong way. They're *fighting* the fat. Fat is an enemy to be obliterated. Jillian Michaels has built a brand around being the drill sergeant with (we're meant to believe) a heart of gold.

Oh sure, I get it. It's supposed to be tough love. And these contestants think they *need* this unforgiving approach, because they feel they've failed so monumentally already. They've bought in to the idea that everything they are is all wrong, and that it's *all their fault.* It's never the fault of biology or genetics or Madison Avenue or Big Food or the wily weight loss industry or the media. They believe their innate weakness is The Problem, and that they deserve to be tortured as a result. It's sad, because when you think that way (as unfortunately, so many fat people do), it doesn't occur to you to be gentle with yourself. And gentleness may be just what these self-flagellating fat people need most.

Yes, believe it or not, gentleness can be a very effective approach to achieving lasting change. In this fat lady's humble opinion, we need to declare a cease-fire on ourselves. We need to lay down our arms and say, "No more fighting"—I am *where* I am, I am *who* I am, and I am *whole*. Sometimes change can only happen when the pressure is off.

I wasted a lot of years believing myself incapable of anything athletic, and so I sat back on my butt and never tried.

But a Christmas gift from an optimistic ex and a decision to move to a beach town changed everything.

You see, an old boyfriend gave me a lovely red beach cruiser bicycle, complete with a wicker basket and a pretty flower-patterned bell. It sat in basement storage in my former Manhattan apartment building for about eight years, rusting. I believed I was too weak to hold myself up, that my butt was too big to sit on the seat, the streets too crowded with unforgiving traffic to make it safe for a trembling wreck of a beginner like me.

Upon moving to an idyllic oceanfront community in New Jersey, where leisurely bicyclists on cheerful pastel cruisers is an uplifting, everyday sight, I decided to climb aboard the old red bike and give it another try.

Yes, it hurt at first. My legs were stiff and unsteady. And in a bona-fide biblical-type miracle, my bicycle seat managed to locate bones buried deep within my abundant ass and pressed them to a point of pain.

But there were also intoxicating oceanic breezes that cleansed me as I rolled through them, feeling like a sun-burned infant diving with the grace of a porpoise into a pool of cool milk, my soul sighing.

I wanted to do it again.

And there was *adventure* in this biking thing! There was curiosity — *satisfied*! Surrounding towns became increasingly familiar as I sailed down little-known side streets, past impeccable art deco mansions and shabby seaside bingo halls lost in time. I discovered farmer's markets and yard sales. And I felt like I could fly.

I went back and rode again.

I used to have moments when I thought to myself, *But I'm not* obsessed *enough with biking for it to make a real impact on my health or well-being. It can't be helping me — it's not* hard *enough!*

However, my legs don't hurt anymore when I ride. And I can ride three towns away and back without feeling like I need an all-day nap to recover. These are indicative of progress, are they not? Of an improved level of fitness?

And isn't any improvement still worthwhile? Don't lots of little improvements eventually add up to big ones?

So maybe I don't have to be "obsessed." Maybe I don't need to be a Gatorade-chugging fanatic in clingy, streamlined shorts. If I never sign up for a hip and happenin' road race for any kind of cure, it'll be A-OK. I believe it's still possible to be happy and healthy and live a long life without changing one's status from geek to jock. Yes, finally, I believe this! After thirty-something years, I have seen there *is* joy in movement!

And maybe if I get in better shape, I'll find joy in even *more* kinds of movement! Who knows? I always dreamed of taking up fencing — inspired by Inigo Montoya in *The Princess Bride*. And when I practice, I want to wear a red sash at my waist. I doubt I'll make it into a Nike commercial with all the would-be Olympic hot bods, but you never know. Look for a chubby girl with a sword or a rickety red bike with a book in its basket, encouraging you warmly to "just do it."

OUT ON A LIMB

As recently as a year ago, I still had a major body hang-up. Until then, I avoided all clothes that bared my legs.

Even in the late 1980s, when I was at my lowest adult weight, I refused to show off my legs. I believed the white fish-belly skin on the backs of my calves and thighs made them look huge and swollen. It limited my wardrobe choices and forced me to find creative ways to work around my "misfortune." Ironically, I was into wearing shorts in those days, but always with opaque tights underneath. I believed the tights were slimming to my legs. I had suede shorts, leather shorts, tartan wool shorts, and wore them all neatly belted at the waist with a funky shirt tucked in. I amassed an impressive collection of tights, which for a time became something of a personal trademark. I had argyle tights, polka-dot tights, tights with human leg bones screenprinted on them, floral tights, Christmas tights, lacy tights. My boyfriend at the time groused, "What's the matter with you, you never show your friggin' legs!"

And I remember around the same time, being in a mall with an acquaintance—Kendra, a woman on the staff of a magazine for which I was also a writer. We stopped on our way to a meeting so she could look at shoes. I remember glancing down at her fat calves, their size and shape obvious in a pair of tight black leggings. I thought, *Dear God, I know I'm prone to thick calves but please,* please *don't ever let mine get as bad as Kendra's!*

In later years, when my calves came to be thicker than Kendra's ever were, I wouldn't wear anything but long pants. No shorts, no dresses, no clam-diggers. Not even ankle-length skirts, because when you walked briskly, sometimes they flipped up from the bottom and a passerby could potentially glimpse a "cankle."

I can't exactly feel *ashamed* of the way I used to feel, because it was a natural consequence of being taught to self-hate. It was hammered into my spongy brain since childhood, impossible to avoid. It was a stepping-stone to feeling as accepting as I do today. But I do *regret* that I ever had to feel that way at all, about myself and about other women.

Sometimes women I admire can disenchant me by needlessly taking a verbal axe to another woman. I remember reading an anecdote about Bette Davis that stuck with me, first because I've been self-conscious about my legs most of my life, and second because I'm a big fan of Davis. It was the 1940s and she was at a Hollywood party when a man and his date entered the room. The date was a woman with thick calves. Someone speculated on the woman's age and Davis quipped, "Well, why don't you just cut off one of her legs and count the rings?"

We didn't just begin passing this hatred along yesterday.

These days I expose my legs freely, completely bare, and feel better about myself in clothes than I did when I was thin.

It took a long time to find this happy body image. And it didn't occur all at once, either. It was a gradual discovery, like an archaeologist working away at a plot of Arizona desert with a toothbrush and uncovering one precious shard of ancient pottery every six months. I didn't wake up one morning, toss the covers from my fat body, and exclaim, "Wow! Look at this bod! I am sooooo comfortable with every inch of it, I think I'll go put on a bikini and parade up and down the nearest highway median. Look out, turnpike drivers! You're about to take the exit to paradise!"

One day, I learned to like the look of my body as a whole in my underwear, taking private pictures of myself in my apartment. Later, I got comfortable with my double chin and gave myself permission to wear turtlenecks, which I used to think drew attention to my fleshy jawline. I said "to hell with it" and started wearing turtlenecks because they felt cozy to me on cold winter days. They felt good to *me*. It mattered more how I felt, than how someone else felt *about* me.

Even later I gave myself permission to wear jeans, something I hadn't done since the early '90s. I'd avoided them because I thought the clinging, pale denim of washed-look jeans highlighted the thickness of my thighs. But there are just certain days that call for a good, scruffy pair of jeans, such as when taking an autumn stroll through Central Park and meandering off the path to kick through piles of leaves. It hurts to realize that for years, I tossed aside so many authentic parts of myself and dressed like an old lady instead, just because I was trying to bandage over my body parts. Because I was trying to protect other people from my appearance. But the very people I was trying to protect — the most judgmental among us — were the people whose approval I wanted the least, though by wrapping myself up, I was only perpetuating the idea that larger, curvier, lumpier, thicker, softer bodies aren't meant to be seen. The more we show a variety of bodies and the more we show ourselves being relaxed with our own "imperfect" bodies, the less taboo and imperfect they will seem to others.

Besides, every fat girl who moves fearlessly through society wearing exactly what she wants, refusing to hide herself away in shame, refusing to be miserable, refusing to sacrifice feeling pretty right where she is, gives other fat girls confidence to do the same. Just as I found body acceptance in stages, there are women everywhere dwelling in stages that precede mine. Maybe you're one of them. Maybe you miss wearing things that make you feel good. Maybe you've never known what it is to dress the part of who you truly are inside. You may be playing it safe, covering yourself up because you fear ridicule. Maybe your own family, even your spouse, would be ready with criticism if you bared your legs or arms, if you wore a shorter blouse or tucked in your shirts. Maybe you dare not wear a hat or a rich color or high heels because you don't want to call attention to yourself. Maybe you want to break out and be free—but you're scared. I was once, too.

I owe it to one cute jersey dress for taking me by the hand and gently leading me through the next phase of self-acceptance. I spied it in a department store. It was my size and knee length. It was cheap and I liked it too much to leave it behind on the rack, so I took it home, thinking I'd just keep it, pull it out of the closet and look at it now and then, try it on and play dress-up with it. I figured I could even wear it like a tunic with pants.

When I finally did wear it in public, that's exactly what I did—paired it with pants and did a Bea Arthur–as–Maude thing with it, very Eastern looking.

But as I undressed later that night, I dared to look at myself in the mirror, without pants. Just me, my legs, and the knee-length dress.

I'd noticed this kind of dress was becoming popular. It was available in plus sizes. I knew, because I'd seen the likes of it on the Web sites of plus-size merchants and in their mail-order catalogs. I'd seen it on the curvy mannequins at the plus-size store in the mall. I'd seen fat women wearing this type of dress in public, with strappy high-heeled sandals, carrying coordinating handbags. I no longer looked upon other fat women the way I'd looked upon Kendra two decades ago. I didn't scrutinize these dress-wearing women and their naked, pudgy limbs and feel pity or hatred. I admired them. I didn't invent body acceptance. Over time, I learned it from women like them, from their courageous example.

When the weather grew warm, I wore the dress as a dress. No pants. That's right, I was gleefully pantless, my big white calves lighting up the world. I wore sexy red patent leather sandals and strutted the whole ensemble into a restaurant. I dared to walk from my table to the restroom on the opposite end of the dining room, passing a hundred other diners, and nothing tragic happened in my world. People didn't faint midbite and slump in their chairs to the crumb-covered floor, or choke on their lobster bisque at the sight of me. The hostess didn't rush to my table and repossess the bread basket. If anybody laughed, I didn't notice. If they laughed, they were officially acting like childish jerks, and why would I let childish jerks get in the way of my fun? I was a woman in a pretty dress, and dammit, I was going to enjoy that.

The cheap jersey dress stirred in me something I hadn't felt since my early twenties. I *wanted* to go shopping. For dresses. Short dresses. And for shoes to go with those dresses.

One afternoon in a discount store I stumbled upon a collection of dresses that looked like something turn-of-the-century orphan girls would wear, like costumes for the cast of *Annie*. Still others resembled Victorian nightgowns. These were the kinds of clothes I'd seen on *Masterpiece Theatre* and in any number of Shirley Temple movies and about which I'd grumbled aloud, "If I could get away with it, I'd totally dress like that, every day, in public." I snatched up one of each—hallelujah, they came in *my size*!—and started tramping around New Jersey looking like an overgrown Bowery street urchin in pigtails. I may have appeared strange to some, but I liked the way I looked. I felt more like my true self than I'd ever felt in a pair of dark polyester-blend pants, hiding away my legs and sweating behind the knees at the height of summer.

Long before I came to enjoy my fat legs, my little sister had a jump on me.

"What do you think, Mom?"

Meg was dressed up for a function at her high school. She stepped into the kitchen modeling a breezy cream-colored dress hemmed to the knee and a pair of sandals with chunky wooden soles. I happened to be visiting from New York, where I lived with my then-fiancé.

My mother took a drag on her cigarette before answering. "Those shoes make your legs look thick," she stated. "You should wear something with a flat sole; it'll slim out your calves." Meg leaned over from the waist and examined her legs, sticking one leg out at an angle and pointing her toes, twisting the leg to study its contours. I had those same thick legs, only longer because I was taller than Meg.

"They do seem to play up your calves," I added "helpfully," echoing my mother. Mom taught me everything I knew about de-emphasizing my "flaws" through careful fashion choices. Although she once tried to convince me that wearing all-black made me look fatter rather than slimming me down, "because it highlights your shape against the background of everything. You'd look thinner if you wore all white." I decided to think for myself on that point and dressed like a nun anyway.

Meg straightened up and without looking at any of us, she shrugged and said, "Well, I like these shoes," and exited the room with gentle dignity. She did not change what she wore. And I think she felt pretty.

Just as body acceptance didn't begin with me, encouraging self-hatred didn't originate with my mother. She was just another dupe in an endless chain of hypnotized mothers and daughters. *This is beautiful; this isn't.* Why haven't more women stopped to ask, "Hey, wait a minute—why *aren't* thick legs just as beautiful as slim ones? Why *can't* I wear thick-soled shoes if I have thick calves? Who says? And why do they get to be right?"

I hope you'll be willing to go out on a limb and start asking. I promise you won't be alone. Lots of us are already out here.

PART THREE

LIVING LARGE

Why always "not yet"? Do flowers in spring say "not yet"?

—Norman Douglas

BOYS WHO SAID YES

Boys weren't clamoring to ask me out in my high school. So I started asking them.

My first foray into a Sadie Hawkins approach to life was with my favorite busboy at Mario's. Mario's was an Italian restaurant in a strip mall in Long Island, New York, where we lived at the time. I had a crush on the tall, chalky guy with the canary yellow hair that fell in a glossy shock over one eye, suitable for those moody, devil-may-care tosses of the head that dominated music videos of the day. I regarded him as a boyish cross between David Bowie and Martin Frye, the lead singer of the English pop group ABC.

I didn't know my bus-boyfriend's name, so I made one up. He couldn't remain nameless—I had to call him *something* in my imagination. So I called him David Bensimon.

During the summer between ninth and tenth grades, my parents took my siblings and me to Mario's for dinner every Saturday night, and I watched with unblinking intensity as David Bensimon whisked away half-eaten hunks of lasagna and replaced errant forks with elegant speed.

And oh, how my friends rolled their eyes whenever we left the movies and the question of where to eat arose. With painful predictability and a piteous, hopeful little hop, I

would chirp, "Ooh, ooh, can we go to Mario's? David Bensimon is working tonight!" and with a chorus of heavy
sighs they'd give in, "Ohhhh-*kaaaaay*...."

On my very first day of high school (which in my school
district was tenth grade, not ninth), lo and behold, I spot-
ted David Bensimon *himself* walking toward me through a
thronged corridor, head and shoulders above the herd. You
couldn't miss that bright, sunny hair.

I was astonished. I told Lisa, Dara, Shane, Kathy, anybody I thought might care, that I'd seen David Bensimon
in the hallway of *our school*!

Minutes after the dismissal bell, we were standing
among the gaggle of students gathered by the school
buses—Kathy, Lisa, and I. David Bensimon was inches
away, idling in a red windbreaker with a backpack
over one shoulder. In a husky whisper, I announced my
intention.

I psyched myself into a feeling of invincibility. I lifted
my chin and rolled my shoulders back, because it helped.
A surge of adrenaline buzzed just beneath the surface of
my skin, and my muscles grew warm. In my mind, an excuse to introduce myself to David Bensimon rapidly took
shape. Then I sidled over to my target, although in my
head I felt like I was running through a dark cave without
stopping, just to get to the light. If I stopped running, I
might actually feel afraid. So inwardly I barreled forward
while outwardly I made my relaxed approach and said:

"Hi. My name is Kim and I'm taking a photography
class with Mr. Myer, and I think you'd make a great male
model. Do you mind if I take your picture?"

It was true, I *was* taking Photography 101, and from
my green nylon Benetton shoulder bag I whipped out my
mother's 35-millimeter camera to emphasize the fact.

David Bensimon chuckled shyly.

"A male model? Really?"

"Yes! So, what do you say? Just a couple of shots. Ready?"

I started snapping away, not waiting for permission.

"Don't look at the camera," I instructed. "Look off into that line of trees over there. Great!"

Those pictures still reside inside my high school scrapbook.

"What's your name?" I asked, replacing the lens cap with the nonchalance of a pro.

"David," he said. Not to my surprise, and yet to my total shock. I threw a look at Kathy. His name really *is* David!

"David, do you have a girlfriend?"

Again, he smiled bashfully and his freckled cheeks pinked.

"Uh . . . no."

"Well, listen, maybe we could go to the movies sometime. Can I give you my number?"

Out of the corner of my eye, I could see Kathy and Lisa mouthing "Oh my *God*!" and falling against each other in disbelief.

I scribbled my name and number on a scrap of paper and David wrote on half, ripped it off, and gave it to me.

"Well, thanks," I said. "I have to get my bus, but I'll see ya later!"

I started moving back in the direction of my posse as I unfolded the jagged little slip of paper in my hands. In neat but boyish handwriting, the name read *David Brickston*.

"No way! No way!" I whispered hotly. "You guys, his name is *David Brickston*! Can you believe that? Can you believe how close that is to David Bensimon?"

Lisa and Kathy were underwhelmed by the coincidence but in awe of my nerve.

"Kim!" Lisa exhaled. "I don't believe you!"

"Kim, gah, that took a lot of nerve," added Kathy. "And he's cute, too. I could never have approached a guy like that."

You might think I had iron-clad confidence to have done what I did. But in fact, my self-esteem was in the toilet. After all, I was a fat, frizzy-haired freak with gappy teeth. I really had no reason to believe I'd be successful in asking out any boy, particularly one as cute as David Bensimon/ Brickston.

My brazen approach by the buses was quite the exception. As a rule, I tried to remain as invisible as possible. It seemed I wore a peculiar bull's-eye that only the nastiest kids could see. "Honey, you have something on your back..." a compassionate teacher would say, guiding me into the nearest bathroom to help me wipe the huge mass of phlegm from my coat.

By walking with my head down most of the time, I couldn't know for sure that I was going completely unnoticed. But I assumed that if I was really someone special, the world would let me know. Admirers would run up to me and throw their arms around me and pull me into a sphere of popularity and universal acceptance. Friends would flock to my side. Boys would step right into my path, *forcing* me to look up, just so they could declare their eternal love.

Fanfare of all kinds happened around you if you were beautiful. If you were thin.

I don't know what clicked inside my brain that made me realize that if I wanted exciting things to happen to me, I'd have to take a more active part. But eventually I understood this. I decided to compensate for being a freak of nature by working extrahard to convince the world I wasn't.

I didn't possess a natural ease around boys. I drew on my experience from junior high, back in Tennessee, before we'd moved to New York. In eighth grade I'd managed to talk fearlessly with good-looking older boys who came to our dances from other schools. Not like a silly, lash-batting butterfly, though, and not with the silken, hypnotic grace of my friend Glory Davis. More like a guy talking to another guy. I noted that I felt at ease this way. I found out which boys my wallflower friends had crushes on and brokered dances for them. Pulling aside the studly subject, I'd say "How ya doin'?" extending a hand. "My name's Kim."

I might occasionally take a dude a little off-guard, but they never responded negatively to my breezy faux-confidence. They'd shake my hand, tell me their name. They didn't quite know what to make of me, and I think that confusion bought me their receptivity, shocked them into acting civil. And as long as they came from another school, they had no way of knowing what an outcast I really was on my home turf.

"Listen, Todd," I'd say, shifting my position so I was standing beside him and leaning my forearm on his shoulder. "Y'see that blonde over there in the pink legwarmers? Name's Becky. Really sweet girl. Look, you would totally make her night if you danced with her, just once. Think you could spare four minutes, say, when the next Journey song comes on?"

And they'd usually do it.

I found a place where I could hold my head up for a few hours at a time and interact with boys. The next logical challenge was to step outside the safety boundary of my buddy-to-buddy approach and try to be seen as a real girl.

I understood on some level that there was virtually no difference between acting beautiful and appearing truly beautiful, as far as other people's perceptions were concerned. At the time, it seemed to me that most people could look at a girl who was an absolute dog, and if she acted like she was Heather Locklear, they totally bought it. I could refer to at least one real-life example of this fascinating phenomenon in Stacey DiNunzio.

Stacey was the reigning queen of the Dirtbags. I've heard of other schools referring to this same community as Metalheads, Headbangers, or just plain Heads (as opposed to, say, Jocks or Punks). The Dirtbags were the kids who listened to heavy metal music, wore leopard-print stretch leggings, and smoked weed under the ramshackle tin roof behind the school (dubbed The Smoke Shack). The Dirtbags accepted their designation without protest. They'd long reclaimed the word.

Stacey DiNunzio was a hard-looking brunette with a weak chin and narrow teeth. She was long and tall, and her limbs looked rubbery to me. There was a hint of poor posture about her shoulders, an osteoporosis-like roundedness for which she seemed too young. She wore more makeup than I'd ever seen on any other girl my age. Her hair looked like a giant spiky pineapple, brittle and tragically oversprayed. She always dressed to the Dirtbag-nines, in elaborately menacing ensembles with spike-heeled boots, mesh and leather, feathers and fringe and studs, all in black and do-me pink.

Stacey DiNunzio entered every room with audacious self-awareness. When she walked through a set of double doors, she didn't pass through one half in the ordinary way. Stacey *burst* through doors, forced them open from dead-center and made a real entrance, like she was David Lee Roth himself taking the stage. I half expected her to jump onto a desk and start playing air guitar. And yes, the Dirtbag boys loved her. Even though, in my fifteen-year-old's estimation, the chick was a total bowwow.

Even if, for a brief moment, a guy suspected Stacey DiNunzio wasn't that attractive, I imagined that something inside of him chose to beat back that impression. I wondered if on some level, in that one doubting moment, he believed the problem was in his own head. A handicap of perception, if you will. Because obviously, the rest of the world—the Dirtbag world, anyway—believed Stacey was steamin' hot shit. Even Stacey. Obviously, everyone else was seeing something he wasn't. He only had to look at the way she carried herself, the way the world reacted to her, to know that *he* was the one with the impairment.

I suspected this quiet scenario was playing itself out every day, somewhere in the universe. And I wanted to be on the same side of the action as the Stacey DiNunzios of the world. What if I could turn my own freakishness on its head? What if I pretended to be beautiful and charming and confident? Would other people positively lick it up? Boys specifically?

David Brickston was my guinea pig.

From the moment my feet started moving in David's direction, to walking away again with his phone number in my hand, I was playing a part. The part of a girl sort of like me, only much, much better.

But feigning confidence with boys was hard to sustain. I could only channel my alter ego intermittently. Because it was an "act," it required energy. It was work. And it could be exhausting. In order for every waking moment not to be tiring, I'd eventually have to break down and be myself.

Sometimes the effort took its toll and I screwed up. It was like I'd strike a frantic pitch inside myself when really I just longed to turn off, go slack, and let the whole act go. Instead, I'd get manic and do or say something foolish. Like when I eventually scared away David Brickston by asking him cheekily from atop his JCPenney bedspread what his favorite part of the female anatomy was. The question, along with the creepy fake giggle, was out of my mouth before I could remember who the heck I was.

That breaking down, that exhaustion from trying to overcompensate for being a natural-born weirdo, made me feel like an even *bigger* weirdo. I must have seemed schizophrenic at times. Poor David Brickston! I wasn't relaxed with myself, so how could I have expected *him* to feel relaxed with *me*?

Soon enough, I bounced back and gave boys another go. This time, I set my sights on a guy named Mark Pantone from my algebra class. He was a lanky kid with longish sandy hair, who reminded me of Stewart Copeland, the drummer from The Police. He liked to draw, and that turned me on because I loved art, too. He was listed in the phone book. So one night, I called him.

His father answered. He called Mark to the phone, "Mark! It's a girl. Kim Brittingham?"

In the background there was frantic whispering, the scraping of chairs against linoleum, hands cupped over the receiver then released again. His father hissed, *"You get over there and take that phone call or . . . !"*

I understood right away. Mark Pantone didn't want to talk to me. He was so appalled, he was probably making all kinds of desperate flailing gestures with his hands and arms, begging his father to lie and say he wasn't home. Maybe he even said, "Ew, it's that fat girl from algebra!"

I promptly concocted a story to save my own face.

After being dragged to the phone by the hair, Mark said hello. And I asked if he'd be willing to join the Art Club, because I was recruiting new members. I told him when the meetings were and asked him to consider stopping by next Thursday. I thanked him cheerfully and hung up the phone. Then I cried. Quietly, so no one outside my bedroom would hear me.

By the time I'd regained my footing yet again, it was near the end of the school year. I was graduating early—it was the end of eleventh grade for me. My family was moving from New York, full-circle back to Philadelphia, and I didn't want to go through being the new kid again just for one lousy year. It wasn't worth it. I talked to a guidance counselor and was able to finagle things so I graduated that year with the seniors.

But our imminent relocation to another state didn't deter me from pursuing another boy. If he turned out to be the great love of my life, then 150 miles wouldn't keep us apart forever. Besides, it seemed incredibly romantic to leave behind a love that *nearly* was. It was the stuff of Whitney Houston ballads. I almost couldn't wait to begin sobbing. It felt so good in my gut—the tensing and releasing of my diaphragm as I cried with imaginary regret. My bottom lip, salty and sweet, awash with my tears, tasted delightful.

He intrigued me. He was in a lot of the same art classes as me, but he wasn't part of the artsy crowd. He was different. He wore nerdy plaid cowboy shirts with pearly buttons and combed his glossy black hair neatly to the side like a Devo helmet, but without the irony. And he was in all the advanced placement classes, so I knew he must be smart. He was at least six feet tall and had serious black eyes that matched his hair. I wanted to know more about him.

I noticed at lunchtime he liked to hide away—far, far back in the most distant corner of the school library, settled into a plastic chair between the very last bookcase and the wall. I found him there reading, and he looked as though he truly didn't want to be bothered.

So one day, summoning all my fake bravado, I went back into the corner and said, "Hi!"

His eyes slid upward from the book page, but he didn't lift his head. "Hi," he said flatly.

"Whatcha readin'?" I asked, channeling a plucky 1930s movie heroine.

And he said something like, "The Physiologicobotanicapseudominaphenal Aspects of the Alteraliteal Atmospheric Plane," and I think I said, "Oh. Okay, well, I'll see y'around."

I asked Patty, a classmate, who he was. I'd seen them riding in a car together—her, him, and her brother. His name was Jason Fulcroft and I learned they were neighbors and had known each other since kindergarten. She seemed excited that I was asking. "He is soooo nice," she volunteered. "Really, he is so sweet, and really smart, too!"

I paid a couple more brief visits to Jason's corner of the library. I pointed out to him that I was in some of his classes and I told him my name, although he didn't offer his. He was stony and minimally responsive. I could see he wasn't in the mood, would never be in the mood, for me.

There were only two more weeks left in the school year. My parents had already moved to Philadelphia, but since I still had school to finish, I struck a deal to stay with my friend Kathy's family until graduation day. Then my parents would drive back to New York, attend the ceremony, and drag me back to Pennsylvania with them.

I was with Kathy and Lisa at the mall when I announced I'd given up on Jason Fulcroft.

"Oh no, that's so sad!" Lisa lamented. "The whole time you were trying to talk to him, I kept thinking, oooh, maybe he'll ask her to the *prom*!"

Kathy gasped. "Oh, wouldn't that be beautiful! You'd get to go to the prom before you move away!"

I wasn't especially sentimental about high school, and

that included the whole concept of prom. In recent weeks my mother had asked me if I'd given any thought to going.

"No," I'd droned in my lowest register. "I couldn't care less about the prom. What a stupid ritual."

She sighed, "Oh, Kim..." and shook her head, as though I didn't know what I was missing. Sometimes I got the feeling she wanted me to be normal in the worst way, to experience all those classic high school moments that maybe she didn't: slumber parties; snapshots framing a vanity mirror of me and my dozen friends in board shorts and bikinis, hamming it up on the beach; boys standing at the front door bearing corsages. The whole thing made me queasy.

But there in the mall, Lisa and Kathy's enthusiasm was contagious.

"Well, it might've been cool," I admitted. "But there's no prom dress in the world that would fit me, or look nice on me."

They shook their heads.

"Kim, that can't be true," Kathy said.

Lisa froze in place and her face lit up. "I have an idea! Let's go into A&S and you can try on some dresses!"

"I don't know..."

"Oh my God, what fun! C'mon, Kim, humor us. Just for fun, let's do it."

I was prepared for a frustrating half hour in a cramped fitting room with five or six dresses that, one after the other, wouldn't slide over my hips, or wouldn't zip, or made me look like a stuffed sausage. I'd break down crying. I'd hate myself for being fat and lumpy, and for being so thoroughly flawed that no effort I ever made to change resulted in success. Fat, ugly, and trapped in it.

We entered the formals department and Lisa made a beeline to a knee-length dress with a black velvet bodice, a black taffeta skirt full like a balloon shade, and a pretty red ribbon belt.

She pushed the hangers back and forth, then lifted out a dress from the back of the rack. "Do you think you could wear a fourteen?"

Even before I emerged from the fitting room, I knew what to expect. We had a winner. It was a miracle. I emerged timidly onto the sales floor and Kathy and Lisa gasped.

"Oh, Kim. That looks *so* nice on you!"

The dress had a dropped waist that seemed to disguise the extreme pear-shape of my body. The poufy hem drew the eye from my thick calves.

"You need to get this dress because that guy *is* going to take you to the prom," Kathy declared. "The dress will bring you luck."

"Come on, every time I go back into that corner, he looks like he wants to rip my face off," I argued. "Besides, I don't have any money."

"Call your mom and ask her," ordered Lisa.

I changed back into my street clothes and allowed myself to be ushered to a phone booth outside of Orange Julius, where a handful of quarters connected me to my grandmother's house in Philadelphia, where my parents were staying.

I was prepared for my mom to be unbearably cloying. To coo into the phone, wanting to rush me out and buy matching shoes.

"Mom, it's me. I'm at the mall with Kathy and Lisa, and well...is there any way I could get eighty dollars for a dress? It's a...a *prom* dress. And it doesn't even make me look fat!"

I braced myself for a bunch of sappy, nosy questions about the boy, the dress.

"You want eighty dollars for a *dress*?" she said acidly. "I don't have *eighty fucking dollars*! What are you, crazy?"

Two flames leapt out of thin air and set my cheeks ablaze. "Well, it's just that this boy might want to take—"

"I've got twenty-five fucking cents left to my name, kiddo!" she shrieked. "You hear that? Not even two god-damned quarters to rub *together,* and *you* want eighty dollars for a *dress*?"

"Never mind!" I spat and slammed down the earpiece. My eyes stung and a bubble rose inside my throat.

"What did she say?" Lisa asked cautiously.

"Nothing," I said, wiping away the hot tears from my eyes. "Let's just forget it. The prom isn't going to happen. He wouldn't have asked me anyway."

I was already finished with the schoolwork that mattered, so I decided to play hooky the entire last week of school. I didn't see the point in going, especially since Jason wasn't responding favorably. He wasn't going along with my plan to leave behind the boy who could've been. The decision to wimp out on the last five days of school was self-protective, I think. I didn't want the melancholy of an entire week of winding down and saying good-bye. I wanted to pretend I was just finished with the place, had no emotion about it whatsoever, and was just biding my time until I could pick up my crummy diploma and be on my way.

I showed up for graduation, threw my yellow nylon cap into the air just for conformity's sake, not with any real enthusiasm. My parents came with my grandmother. They brought me flowers. I gave some farewell hugs to teachers and friends. Then Patty came rushing up to me.

"Where have you *been*?" she asked. "Jason Fulcroft has been looking *all over* for you, for a *week*! He's been asking everybody if they know you. I've never seen anything like it in all the years we've lived next door to each other. He was actually grabbing people at random in the hallway and asking, 'Hey, do you know Kim Brittingham?' I found your phone number in the phone book and gave it to him, but he said it was disconnected. Kim, he wanted to take you to the prom!"

I was shocked.

It was so deliciously romantic.

A few days after settling into our new house in Philadelphia, I made a polite phone call to Jason, saying I was sorry he couldn't find me and thanking him for trying.

There was such a curious duality in me then—a nagging sense that I was "all wrong," co-existing with an inner spirit that nudged me to try something anyway, even if I was terrified of failure. Some of that duality is still there today. The woman who looks in the mirror and once in a while still sees a swollen, matronly slob pushes through the crazy-talk and speaks her mind, goes on national television, stands before audiences, and wears short dresses anyway. I make a concerted effort to silence that self-hating voice, because I know it's not my own. It's the voice of others outside of me, others less enlightened who, over the years, tried to make me feel bad about myself for their own twisted, selfish, unwholesome reasons. When that voice does shout loud enough to still be heard, I'm able to dismiss it more easily than I could when I was a teenager. I think the voice knows I don't respect it.

I remain dismayed that as a young girl I sought so much validation from *adolescent boys;* that I allowed my self-worth to be measured by the attention they gave me. I'm just glad I was so hell-bent on a glamorous future, because I did everything in my power to avoid pregnancy, disease, foolish breathless elopements, and imprisonment. A girl in my needy emotional state could've wound up in a number of bad places.

I think most of us long for romantic and sexual interaction, and there's certainly nothing wrong with that. It's human nature to want to love and be loved. I just feel sad that so many girls and women, fat or thin, look to their individual appeal as sexual beings for a sense of happiness, importance, and completeness. We're already complete and important. We've already got everything we need within us to be happy, even standing alone. When we realize this, it frees us to pursue what truly intrigues us about this life, and ironically, *that's* when we become the most attractive. When other people — whether they're potential romantic interests or just future friends — see us operating from a place of personal passion, they recognize us for the individual powerhouses that we are, and they want to be closer to it. They want to be closer to *us*.

When I stopped needing romantic attention so badly, I relaxed into my true self.

But I will say this for all the boys I ever chased who said yes: they taught me that not everyone hates a fat girl.

Sure, sometimes people are narrow-minded nitwits. Like this guy Kurt I dated in my early twenties. We worked in the same mall. I was a picture framer; he worked in the camera shop. The guy was positively goo-goo-eyed over me. I was on the lower end of my weight then. I thought he was nice enough, but I was never quite as excited about him as he was about me. He went away to school for a while, and when he returned he was anxious to see me. I met him at a restaurant. As he approached me, his face was strange, his eyes wide. His body language was rigid and robotic. He seemed remote. Over dinner I asked if something was bothering him.

He began stiffly, dropping his head forward so his voice passed low over the surface of the table in short, hushed jerks. "Well, you know that I...to me, you were always, like...the ultimate."

"The ultimate?"

"Yeeeeah," he continued. "In my mind, no one could ever be as...as attractive as you."

It could've been everything a girl hoped to hear from a guy, if it wasn't delivered so haltingly and with such hard, appalled eyes. I knew there was a "but" coming. A big butt.

"I see," I said. "But I've gained a lot of weight since you last saw me, and you're shocked, right?"

He nodded slowly, his neck tight. "Yyyyyyes."

"Uh-huh," I continued, conversationally. But I was hurting inside. In spite of the fact that I didn't give that big a crap about the wiry little creep. "And you were all jazzed to see me, but now that I'm sitting before you like this, I'm not the goddess you used to think I was. And you just can't handle the disparity. Your fantasy has been shattered. Correct?"

He nodded again, slowly. "Yyyyyes," he admitted without shame.

A pedestal crumbled beneath my weight. I stood swiftly, just in time. I wasn't going to wind up on the ground, rolling around in the rubble of this guy's hollow ideal. I managed to excuse myself without shedding a tear. I let it come when I was out of sight.

The good news is, there *are* boys who say yes. Boys who are receptive. Boys who are made of richer stuff. They're capable of seeing past body mass index to the whole person. Some of them even *prefer* a chunkier chick.

The world is full of people. Lots of people, and among them you *will* find kindred spirits who are willing to accept you as you are. Not just accept, but *celebrate* who you are. We find our advocates out in the wider world, and they help clear a space for us to be ourselves without apology, and they give us the courage to stand up for ourselves when necessary.

One final lesson from the boys who said yes: they showed me that persistence pays. They taught me to keep asking. Ask for what you want. Keep going for it. Accept from the outset that there *will* be rejection. And when it happens, you might cry into your pillow, and that'll be okay. The important thing is to bound out of bed the next morning and try again. Because eventually, you get what you want. Whether it's in love or career or anything else, keep asking, because eventually, you get a yes.

FAT AUNT PHYLLIS

Sometimes when I took a second helping of mashed potatoes at the dinner table, one of my parents would snidely ask, "Do you want to be like Aunt Phyllis when you grow up?"

It used to hurt my feelings. My little brother and sister giggled, as they understood they should. Daddy made a funny about fat Aunt Phyllis. He made a funny about Kim, and Kim was always fun to laugh at. "Dramatic" Kim, "Sarah Bernhardt." A child whose extreme emotions—sorrow, worry—provided reliable knee-slapping entertainment for a family that changed addresses and schools, on average, every three years. My foolish existence gave everyone a sense of consistency.

I remember dropping the spoon noisily back into the bowl and hanging my head low over my plate. My face was suddenly weighty with the mounting tension of unshed tears. The whitish yellow mound on my plate blurred into a pale abstract. I was always on the tall side for my age, and I was no waif, so when I rose abruptly from my chair, it tipped violently and clattered against the kitchen wall. I stormed to my bedroom, my legs stiff but quick. I fell onto the bed and cried mournfully into the unsympathetic polyester bedspread, my heart cracking apart—not

for my own sake or for the sake of the reconstituted spuds
I'd left behind. I was crying for my aunt Phyllis.

My sweet, embraceable aunt Phyllis, whose ample chest
seemed to emit rays of late-June sun. I could actually feel
it when she pressed me to her. She was The Fat Aunt, and
as a child I was conditioned to think of her that way — as
huge. A ridiculous giant, a shapeless being, although in retrospect she was probably no fatter than I am today. She
had an impish little-girl's face and a deep, rasping laugh
that made everyone else laugh when they heard it. She had
soft hands, and she smelled like solace — like bread from
the oven.

Aunt Phyllis was my mother's sister, and they were
once the best of friends. They grew up together, the two
girls closest in age in a family of seven children, trudging
through childhood and adolescence, shoulder-to-shoulder,
in charity rags. I used to love hearing their anecdotes from
high school, and from the summer camp where they and
others like them — the poorest of the poor — were bused
from the inner city for fresh air and wholesome activity. I asked my mother to tell me — just one more time,
Mom! — about the time my uncle Ed, their oldest brother
and father-figure, caught them on a street corner wearing
lipstick. He chased them home, bellowing all the way for
them to "wipe that garbage off your faces, you look like a
couple of trollops!" As my mother and Aunt Phyllis clattered up the steps to their second-floor apartment, tripping
over each other in a black hole of adrenaline, their eyes met
and they found time to wonder aloud, "What's a trollop?"

I loved my aunt Phyllis, and I thought my mother loved
her, too. But these remarks made me feel betrayed on my
aunt's behalf. They made me want to haul off and smack
my mother clean across the face. "How *dare* you?"

My mother used to have to buy me specially sized jeans

during my preteen years—Huskies from Sears—and one day as I fidgeted in her wake through the girl's department, she sighed, "You keep eating the way you do, and you'll end up like Aunt Phyllis. You don't want that, do you?" My jaw stiffened. My lower teeth slid uncomfortably against my upper teeth; my nostrils flared. This time, I would speak up.

"Mom, don't you love Aunt Phyllis?"

She didn't look me in the eye. I watched her face closely. Her lower lip went slack. With great concentration, she slid clothes hangers around on a circular chrome garment rack, *squeak, squeak, squeak.*

"Of course I do," she said dully.

Poor Aunt Phyllis, I thought sadly, my eyes stinging. I wondered if she was aware of the limits of her own sister's esteem. Did she understand that the warm spectrum of familial love was restricted in her case? Did she suspect the things that were routinely said about her with a smirk over meatloaf?

Maybe she did. Maybe it's why she chose to live hundreds of miles away from her mother and siblings. Maybe it's why we rarely saw her at Christmastime. It used to disappoint me, year after year: "No, Phyllis isn't coming for the holidays, but she sent this package." She was so whimsical and creative. She composed and mailed poems and stories to be read aloud on Christmas Eve. She made the most clever gifts out of whatever materials she had on hand. One year she fashioned a pocketbook for me out of a pair of her old jeans, using the butt pockets on each of the bag's two sides, and repurposing the waistband as a shoulder strap. She hand-embroidered funny messages into the denim with red and white thread, like *Hey, you! Keep your phalanges off of Kim's bag!!!*

Over the years, my aunt Phyllis consistently coupled with black men, and it was a sore subject in our family. First there was my uncle Carl, the one and only man my aunt Phyllis ever married. They eventually separated and she went on to live with other black men, and he with another woman. Oddly enough, he refused to give my aunt a divorce because he was a devout Catholic. At least that's how it was explained to me.

When I was a little girl of three and four, I adored my uncle Carl. He was as skinny as a stick figure, all elbows and knees, with the whitest teeth I'd ever seen and skin like the bittersweet baker's chocolate Mom kept in the pantry. More than once she had to remind me it was "not for eating, it'll make you sick."

My uncle Carl and I shared a private language. The words didn't mean anything, but we didn't tell anyone else that; we let them think we understood each other. When chattering away in gibberish, we made equal efforts to modulate our voices, as though asking questions and answering them, creating conversational music.

"Bluh-bluh BLOO-bluh ooba duh-bluh?"

"Ohhhh! Bluh-duh-bluh DOO-buh ooh-bluh doo-bah!"

It was Aunt Phyllis who likened me to the little girl in Henry Wadsworth Longfellow's nursery rhyme, because of the single ringlet of hair that always fell between my eyebrows:

> There was a little girl,
>   Who had a little curl,
> Right in the middle of her forehead.
>   When she was good,
>   She was very good indeed,
> But when she was bad she was horrid.

For Christmas one year, Aunt Phyllis and Uncle Carl gave me a book of nursery rhymes, and on the page with the verse about the girl with the curl, there was a line drawing of a little pale-haired girl who, like me, had a shock of hair looped over on itself in the center of her forehead. And beside it in blue ink, in my aunt's handwriting, was an arrow pointing toward her, and this:

KIM!

It was Uncle Carl who taught me how Olympic runners get into position to sprint. He also showed me how to dance The Bump, and how to blow a bubble with bubble gum.

"You've got to chew it 'til it's good and soft," Uncle Carl coached. "Now stretch it out across your tongue — yep, that's good — and then blow air down your tongue and fill it out like a balloon."

"Make sure she doesn't choke on that, Carl," somebody warned.

I settled myself on Aunt Phyllis's lap and tried so very hard, chewing, gnashing, blowing flatulent air across my bottom lip and spreading holes through the gum.

"Don't worry, just keep practicing. In fact," he said, jumping out of his seat like a long brown rabbit and taking a camera from his bag, "I'm going to sit right here on the floor in front of you with the camera in my hand. Now you just keep on trying, as long as it takes. As soon as you blow a real bubble, I want you to raise your hand high in the air and wave it around, like this!" He thrust his long, slender arm above his head and waggled his pink, brown-lined palm. "When I see that, I'll pick the camera right up and take a picture. Your very first bubble!"

I chewed and blew until my lips and jaw were sore, and then, finally, it happened. I could feel it! A bubble! Not a big one, but it was *real*, a genuine bubblegum bubble taut

with my breath and sitting fatly on my slick lips. My hand
flew into the air, my uncle lifted his camera and bathed me
in flashbulb blue.

Some years later, I asked my mother, why *did* Aunt
Phyllis only date black guys? I loved digging for dirt.

"It's a self-esteem issue," my mother sighed with weary
authority. "Sometimes when a white woman like your aunt
is so heavyset, and doesn't see her own value, she'll give
up on getting herself together. Instead, she'll settle for a
black man. It's because she doesn't believe she can do any
better. She'd rather be with a black man than be alone."
She toked on her cigarette and its tip surged red, then
went black. And then, with resigned gravity, as if it was
a shame: "Your aunt does exactly what she wants to do."

Despite the fact that Aunt Phyllis kept a friendly distance, I did get a chance to visit her on her own turf, but
only once. She was living in rural Virginia, in a motel
room with her boyfriend at the time, a long-distance truck
driver. I was about fourteen, and members of the family
had converged on Richmond for a cousin's wedding. I rode
along with my grandmother, another aunt, and an uncle
to visit Aunt Phyllis. After a stretch of bleak highway and
a long, wooded country road, we pulled into a clearing
of wheatlike, trodden yellow grass. A bone-dry concrete
fountain with flaking white paint stood in the foreground
of a shabby single-story motor lodge. As we rolled past the
fountain, I could see it was filled with half a dozen lanky
black boys playing in the empty basin. There was a country store beside the motel, a gray clapboard structure with
a sagging porch. I remembered my uncle saying that Aunt
Phyllis worked in the store part-time. "She sits there at
the counter all day and eats up the guy's stock. One package of Twinkies and Ring Dings after another, hour after
hour. I don't know why the guy doesn't fire her." Every-

one always made Aunt Phyllis's life sound so miserable.
"She wrote a children's book once," my mother said. "She
sent it to all the big publishers in New York but they told
her it was 'too moralistic.' After that, she just gave up. On
everything."

Aunt Phyllis's black boyfriend wasn't at home when
we came calling. He was out on a job, hauling something
out to the West Coast. The motel room they called home
was a tiny box with a tall ceiling. I remember my aunt
sat camped out in the center of the bed like an empress in
a stained T-shirt, with a cigarette sending smoke signals
up from a nearby ashtray. On a crappy television riding
a rust-spotted cart, soap opera actors moved like ghosts
through a blizzard of static, and dodged black-and-white
lightning strikes of interference; they recited their lines
through tin cans. She cleared spaces on the bed for us to
settle our weight, as there were no chairs. The room was
filled with stacks of moldy cardboard boxes and laundry
hampers filled with all manner of clothes and miscellany.
The smell of sweat and barbecue sauce seemed to hang in
a cone over the room, drifting occasionally from one spot
to another, growing momentarily more intense, then re-
ceding. I couldn't believe she lived this way, but I wasn't
going to let her see my disappointment. I showed her love,
I told her I was happy to see her — and that was the truth.

Maybe Aunt Phyllis *did* have poor self-esteem. I couldn't
know for sure. It wasn't what I wanted for her, but as a
teenager I didn't know how to express that. I wondered
if her boyfriend treated her well. I didn't care that he was
black, or even that he couldn't afford to keep her in more
pleasant surroundings. Family members implied that she
chose to live this way. That she didn't feel entitled to anything cleaner, brighter, more lively or hopeful. There was so

much I didn't know and didn't understand. I didn't know who or what to believe. I didn't know how to directly ask this woman I loved who she was, what she wanted, or if she was happy. I was always being told I was too young to comprehend anything, particularly the things my parents whispered about after long-distance phone calls from family. So I kept my eyes and ears open, and my mouth shut.

When I was in my thirties and seeing a therapist, I expressed worry about my weight.

"I just can't seem to help myself, but I desperately need to stop living this way. I'm just too fat. I'm scared I'm going to get a disease and die young. Before I ever get to make any of my dreams come true."

My aunt Phyllis died of cancer. She was in her fifties. She'd also had at least one surgery when she was even younger than that, but no one explained to me why. I don't know what kind of cancer eventually took her, either. All I know was that she was living in a trailer park when she got sick — "living in some black woman's trailer, with the woman and her kids," my uncle explained. When it was clear my aunt Phyllis was dying, my aunt Mae collected her from the far-flung trailer park and set up hospice for her in a spare bedroom.

"Why are you so convinced you're going to get sick and die?" Gerri, my therapist, wanted to know.

"Because," I sniffed. "Because my aunt Phyllis died. And I'm just like her. She was the fat one in the family. Now *I'm* the fat one. The path is already laid out for me. Like some kind of...I don't know. Family destiny."

Gerri leaned forward in her chair. "Kim, I want you to look at me," she said, peering at me intently. "*You are not your aunt*. Your aunt was her own person. *You* are your own person. And just because she was fat doesn't mean you're going to end up just like her. Your life is *already* much different from hers. Look at you! At the very least, you have the self-awareness to seek therapy, and that's something your aunt was never able to do for herself."

I sat thinking about how everyone always said my aunt just "gave up." I wanted to believe that wasn't true. I didn't buy the whole thing about the interracial relationships being some kind of surrender, but I couldn't help wishing she'd fought a little harder for the things it seemed she'd wanted. At the very least, her children's book. If it was me, I would've gone to my grave with a sheaf of fresh cover letters and a tweaked manuscript in my stiff, dead hands.

"But I don't think this is you talking," Gerri piped up again. "Let's figure out whose voice this is, telling you you're destined to be *just like Aunt Phyllis*."

I didn't get to see my aunt before she passed, but my mother, Aunt Mae, and Uncle Ed were by her side for the entire last week of her life. By telephone, I heard how the morphine caused her to pick at phantom lint on her blanket. I heard that Uncle Carl came and told her through her drug haze, "Phyllis, you're going to meet your children now."

"Her children?" I repeated. "What children?"

"She had two miscarriages," my mother replied casually. "It was years ago, when she was still with Carl."

I didn't even know she'd wanted any children.

"Oh, yeah. Very much," my mother said.

I knew her death was imminent, but when Aunt Phyllis finally departed this world, my own reaction surprised me. My mother called and delivered the news, plainly and softly. And the tears came to my eyes and a needle pricked at my heart, and then my brain seemed to enclose itself stubbornly in a snug box. I became strangely single-minded—there was only one thing I wanted to know, *one thing*.

"Tell me, Mom, tell me," I choked via long-distance, "did she know she was loved?"

"Yes, hon, she knew."

"No," I snapped. "I mean, did you *tell* her?"

"Yes, honey. We told her every day."

"But are you sure she heard you?" I sobbed, my voice strained, my throat thick. I didn't see the room around me, I saw nothing, nothing but a blank space like a clean chalkboard that I so desperately wanted to mark with a word of surety. "Was she awake when you told her, did she really know? I just want to make sure she knew she was loved, that's all. That while she was here, she knew she'd been *loved* in this world."

"She knew, Kim. Believe me, she knew."

I trusted it. I had to, if only so I could see again. I let my mother's word be enough.

My mom went on to say that the undertaker wouldn't be there for a while; they were in the middle of a hurricane.

"Mom," I said tentatively, "I know this might sound crazy, but I think Aunt Phyllis left with the hurricane. I think she rode away on it. Like a flying carpet."

Even in her grief, I expected no less from my mother than a hearty laugh and a sigh—"Oh, Kim. Where do you come up with these things?" Instead, her voice was gentle and even. "No. No, that doesn't sound crazy," she said. "After your aunt Phyllis passed, I left her alone in the room and went into the backyard. Your uncle Ed was out

there sitting in a lawn chair, and I sat down next to him.
The wind was starting to pick up, and I looked up into the
tops of the trees that bordered the yard, and I called to her,
'Now you're free, Phyllis. Whip it up! Go on, baby! Whip
it up!' "

FAT IS CONTAGIOUS

There was a time when I rode the public buses of New York City nearly every day, to and from work at least. Overall, my experience showed me that most bus riders prefer to sit rather than stand. That is, unless they have to sit next to a fat person.

I've been on buses that filled to an inhumane capacity, with commuters packed in like desperate refugees or sows to the slaughter. Still, the seat beside me remained empty. I once watched a woman tolerate being wedged between a foul-smelling man with roaming hands and a perspiring giant with a hairy armpit an inch from her face, yet she staunchly refused to collapse comfortably into the seat available at my side. To be fair, she might've been enjoying the feel-up, but judging by her expression of disgust and the dirty looks she kept shooting at me, I think not. Why wouldn't she just *sit*? And what had *I* done to deserve the evil eye? Had I contaminated an otherwise perfectly good seat by situating my deadly girth beside it?

Some people don't even bother to be subtle. One woman attempted to sit beside me and made a big show of squirming uncomfortably before crossing the aisle in a noisy huff. She sat beside a sympathetic stranger with shaking head and rolling eyes, to whom she churlishly complained, "Some people got a lot of nerve!"

I can understand how the seat beside a large person might be viewed as less desirable than one beside a slimmer person, for reasons of bodily comfort. A tiny person might leave the seat-seeker more room to move in his or her own space. Oftentimes I, too, chose to stand when I spied an open seat between two people that looked like it wouldn't comfortably accommodate my large body. I simply didn't want to be squashed in the middle.

What I *don't* understand, however, is those times when seats were at a premium, like during rush hour, and very few people were willing to suck it up and sit next to me in a seat on the *aisle*—that's right, an aisle seat where there was no wedged-between factor. Even I found it infinitely more comfortable to sit in an aisle seat beside another large person, with one of my ass-cheeks hanging over the side, than to *stand* for forty blocks being jerked clumsily to and fro in high-heeled boots.

When it wasn't adults refusing to sit beside me, it was their children, children of four and younger already imbued by the media or their parents with the unarticulated but unmistakable code that fat people are bad. Bad, dirty, poor, stupid, sick. I watched, saddened, as children twisted and whined at their nannies' sides when it was suggested that they take a seat beside me.

Sometimes I actually got to witness the process of this unfortunate indoctrination. I remember an as-yet-untainted child approaching the empty seat beside me and climbing guileless into it, grinning, all cheeks and Chiclet-teeth. Her mother snatched her away and suggested that she sit over *there* instead. When the little girl asked, "Why, Mommy?" her mother was dismissive and uneasy. While my hips and ass may be wide, trust me, they've never bled so far outward that I couldn't accommodate the feathery body of a three-year-old at my side.

The way people act, you'd think fat was contagious.

Over time, I couldn't help wondering what other riders were thinking when they chose not to sit next to me on the bus. At that moment of decision—to sit or not to sit next to the fat girl—were their thoughts crystal clear, like type-writing across their brains? *You don't want to sit next to that fat woman, because (a) she might smell like bratwurst, (b) her excess sweat will rub off on you and stain your good blouse, or (c) it'll be a lot less comfortable than standing.* Or were their thoughts more like a swirling purple vapor of vague collected precepts? *Fat...bad...icky...undesir-able...diseased...avoid...stand.*

Then one afternoon I was inspired to launch an experi-ment, to engage in an act of performance art, of sorts.

I created a fake book cover using my home computer. Some rectangles of color here, a change in font there, a borrowed bar code, some clip art of a cartoon fat woman on a shuddering scale, and *voilà*! I churned out a highly convincing nonfiction book jacket. I wrapped it around a newly purchased biography, and after a little tugging and folding and fun with transparent tape, I held the book out

before me. My heart swelled at the sight of it, my cheeks grew warm. My god. It looked so *real*.

For several weeks, as I rode all over Manhattan, I worked my way through *Fat Is Contagious* (or rather, whatever cleverly cloaked tome I was currently reading), one twenty-minute ride at a time. Even when I appeared completely engrossed in its pages, I was aware of the dozens of people who strained their necks doing double-, triple-, and even quadruple-takes to read and reread its cover. Wherever my book was in clear public view, someone inevitably noticed.

Some people appeared absolutely stunned, mouths comically agape; still others couldn't conceal their absolute horror. Many looked just plain dumbfounded, a little goosed perhaps, and undeniably confused. The looks alone were priceless. Pure entertainment.

Once in a while I received a smile, but I'll never know which ones were pitying my perceived stupidity or, like a particularly handsome man peeking over the top of a *Wall Street Journal* with a knowing twinkle in his eye, seeming to congratulate me on a cleverly executed hoax.

On two separate occasions, I spied women sitting opposite me jotting down the title and author on the back of a phone bill or a drugstore receipt, scrawling hastily between surreptitious glances from beneath an overhang of hair. I wondered, were these women seeking to learn which trendy nutritional supplement would protect them from the perils of infectious fatness? Or were they burning to write a venomous letter to the author, verbose in its feminist ideologies?

One day I overheard a young woman on the bus phoning a friend, making no special effort to keep her voice down: "Cheryl, it's me. Listen. I'm on the 79 bus and I'm sitting across from this woman who's reading a book called *Fat Is Contagious, How Sitting Next to a Fat Person Can Make You Fat*. No, I'm serious. Yes. I know it's mind-boggling. Should I ask? OK, well, can you check Amazon for me?"

One middle-aged man sat beside me, took one good look at the book cover, and literally ran to the back of the bus!

After witnessing a wide variety of entertaining reactions to *Fat Is Contagious,* I finally received one concrete answer to my original question: What are people thinking when they choose not to sit beside me? I got an answer that was true, uncensored, and specific. One woman responded out loud on behalf of everyone who'd ever intentionally avoided, snickered, or sneered at a fat person, giving a real voice to so many of those riders still tethered to the handrails in standee silence. And ironically, it all happened before I'd even managed to pull *Fat Is Contagious* from my messenger bag.

I'd just finished a long day of jury duty and all I wanted was to head home and lose myself in a good book. I climbed onto the bus and sank into a seat on the end of a row of three. A statuesque, capable-looking woman with skin like cocoa powder sat on the other end. I was rummaging in the bag on my lap when I heard a belligerent voice spit, "Excuse me!"

I looked up to see another woman glowering down upon me. I'd classify her as "an older woman," but I couldn't be sure of her age. She had haggard features that might make you believe a woman to be older than she actually is. She was tiny and slight in an oversized coat that hung heavily from her narrow shoulders. Her skin appeared tough and slightly yellow, and the auburn hair that showed from beneath her woolen cap looked brittle and lusterless. She scowled at me through Coke-bottle glasses. I had no idea what she wanted.

"Yes?" I asked.

She pointed to the middle seat. A fringed triangle of my shawl had fallen into it. I reached down to lift it into my lap and she quickly snapped, "Oh, never mind!" She turned to the woman on the other end of the row and spat, "If some people won't lose weight, they should have to pay for two seats!"

To this cranky little woman's dismay, she encountered no support.

"What are you talking about?" the seated woman replied in a melodious Caribbean accent. "There's plenty of room for you in that chair! And what are you saying, lose the weight? There's nothing wrong with this lady! She's just fine the way she is!".

Two plump women sharing a family resemblance and identical ponytail holders sat snugly against each other in seats across the aisle. Their eyebrows shot up beyond their bangs.

"Oh no she di-in't!" they chorused. "Did that lady just say you need to pay for two seats? Who the hell she think she is?"

The self-righteous little woman (I'll call her Ms. Hostility), sensing her viewpoint was unwelcome in the back of this particular bus, moved toward the front. Seconds later, it seemed she'd engaged a stranger in conversation about me, or the stranger did so with her, because I heard Ms. Hostility argue, "Well she should *want to* lose the weight, for her *health*!"

Here I thought I'd been minding my own goddamned business. But just like that, *my weight* had become the sizzling debate-du-jour on the M15 bus.

All right then. If the idea behind this woman's confrontation was that all fat people are hurting themselves with their poor habits, and further, that society should step up and stop this mass self-destruction *by any means necessary* (including malice masquerading as tough love), then why aren't more combatant women hovering over slender people on the bus and berating them for the cigarettes in their shirt pockets, the martinis on their breath, or the excessive stress lingering on their furrowed brows? Why haven't these crusading souls made it their business to fight self-destructive habits across the board? Why aren't bus riders asking other bus riders outright if they have regular checkups and health screenings, and why aren't they glaring down their noses at those who answer in the negative? After all, it's about helping people recognize what's best for their health—right?

The Caribbean lady reached over and put a hand on my arm. "Don't you listen to her," she said in a hush. "She's just jealous. She wants to be young and pretty, like you."

I knew my new friend was right. I wouldn't have traded bodies with that unhappy little troll for any amount of money—and I wanted so badly to *tell her so*. I was growing weary of taking yet-another-hit for the fat team in noble silence. I was tired of letting people skate by saying whatever they felt like about *my private body* anytime, anywhere, in front of anyone—all the while grinding my teeth on overrated grace and eternal forgiveness, replaying in my mind the old Mommyism that I shouldn't lower myself to her level by being just as nasty. My ire was way up, and for good reason. I wanted to say something acidly clever, just plain mean. No, I'm not Mother-frickin'-Teresa, and here's what I was thinking: I wanted to tell her she looked like a rat—a sickly, underfed rat crudely ejected from an overcrowded consumption asylum; a nineteenth-century trash picker just turned out of the workhouse. I wanted to rub it in her face that I was robust and pink and lusty, that I was luscious and plump and smooth as a peach, that I looked like a biblical cherub in the nude, and that she only wished she did.

I wanted to tell her she was the *last* person who ought to comment on the state of a person's health based on the person's appearance. I wanted to thrust a chubby finger in her face and force her to listen as I talked about chunky Olympic softball player Crystl Bustos, and all the fat guys who participate in the annual Big Man Run in Worcester, Massachusetts, with every runner weighing in at a minimum of 200 pounds. How well would Ms. Hostility compete beside the Big Men, and all the other fat runners across the country, male and female, participating in "Clydesdale" and "Filly" running clubs, respectively? I wished Ms. Hostility could meet Jennifer Portnick, a certified aerobics instructor in San Francisco, five-foot-eight and 240 pounds. Would Ms. Hostility be able to keep up with Ms. Portnick? What would she so authoritatively say about the health of Ms. Portnick or Ms. Bustos if she saw one of *them* sitting on the bus?

Ms. Hostility certainly wasn't the first person in history to suggest that fat people should lose weight for their health. Every physician I've ever seen and an uncle with only the best intentions believe the same, and told me so. But why should a complete stranger on a bus be so deeply concerned about *my* health? It's as hackneyed an excuse as they come.

I decided against engaging Ms. Hostility in a debate. Part of me would've relished a cross-examination of her motives, but I was too tired to excavate, too weary to peel away the health argument and find out what bitter, ignorant, heartbreaking belief really lay beneath. I took the high road, but only by exhausted default.

The rotund sisters unleashed some verbal digs on my

behalf. "You're right, she *is* jealous," they piped up. "Just look at her nasty, bony ass."

With easy confidence, I assured them, "What she says can't hurt me."

"You're beautiful, and they're beautiful," the black woman said, gesturing to me and the sisters. "I'm not very skinny myself, but I'm beautiful too."

We all nodded at one another and smiled. "You look stunning. Tall, healthy," I told the kind woman. "We've all got good, sturdy genes. And there's nothing wrong with that."

A growing crowd at the front of the bus forced Ms. Hostility back our way again. She hovered directly above me and glared, stubbornly avoiding the empty seat at my side. I decided to resume what I'd been doing when I was so unpleasantly interrupted the first time. I pulled *Fat Is Contagious* out of my bag and with intentional drama, I widened my eyes mockingly and raised the book slowly, spookily in front of my face, floating it over my nose and mouth. Ms. Hostility and my allies noticed this quiet, curious performance and leaned forward to read the book title. Suddenly, laughter and applause broke out from all sides. The quarrelsome Ms. Hostility made a sour face, turned on her heel, and spurned us for the rest of the ride.

Ms. Hostility and I got off the bus at Union Square. We started moving in the same direction at the same time. Even with a bulky, heavy shoulder bag to bear, I passed her, walking at my usual clip — a pace that tends to be frustratingly fast for most of my friends, fat and thin alike. I wasn't trying to outrun her. I didn't have to. Perhaps her delicate, birdlike physique couldn't support such a vigorous stride. I went about my business, breathing deeply the air of an unusually perfect day; my legs long, sturdy, and sure; my head held high. I looked over my shoulder only once to see if I'd been followed, and I saw Ms. Hostility shuffling toward the doors of Barnes & Noble. Perhaps she was looking to read a copy of *Fat Is Contagious*. For her health.

WHEN THE AVENUE WALKS ON YOU

I have something to tell you, but I don't want you to be upset," Ginger said over the phone. "I just think you should know."

Geez, what could it be? The worst thing I could imagine was that her boss hated my ideas and their client wouldn't want to work with me. Big deal. I'd live.

"What is it, Ginger?"

"The other day when you came into the office, and I told you Kellie was called into a meeting and couldn't see you, well—that was a lie. Kellie *made* me lie."

"Okay..."

"She told me to get rid of you, as quickly as possible. I was given explicit instructions not to deal with you anymore."

"Oh?" *Was it my breath? Too much CK One? Was there paparazzi footage of me at a Duran Duran concert screaming like a little girl, dancing like a slutty banshee, and walking out looking like I'd just stood under the shower? Hey, I know it's unseemly, but there's a time and place for everything.*

"I'm so sorry to say this, but, well... she saw you out in the waiting room and said you were too fat," Ginger confessed. "She said that you weren't worth her time, and that the client would never want to work with you." She paused, then added, "And Kellie is even *more* 'plus' than *you* are!"

"I see," I said temperately. I noted with some pride that my heart did nothing remarkable at this news. Not a skip, not a quirk or a prick or implosion. Just one beat after another. Unsurprised. Unwounded.

"I am so, so sorry," Ginger's voice quivered. "I was put into the most awkward, awful position and I absolutely hated it. In fact, I just walked out yesterday. I quit."

"Good for you."

"I just wanted you to know that I think Kellie made a *huge* mistake. You are incredibly talented. You're poised and beautiful and articulate, and you brought some awesome stuff to the table. I saw your vision, and I think your ideas would've been *phenomenal* for the client."

"Thanks, Ginger. I appreciate that."

"I didn't want you to walk away thinking there was anything wrong with you." (I wasn't thinking that, but I let her continue. It seemed she needed to.) "It's not you—it's them. I just *know* you're going places, I can *feel* it, regardless of what people like Kellie Brown think," she sniffed. "Believe me, Kim, the right people are going to notice you. 5W are assholes, and they're *stupid* assholes. They totally screwed up with you and I think they're going to regret it later."

I nodded to myself and calmly told her that "I think you're absolutely right." I let her apologize again. We agreed to stay in touch. I hung up the phone.

I walked over to my computer. I sat down. I proceeded to blog about the entire thing. And I named names—all but Ginger's.

Ginger worked for a public relations firm in New York City called 5W. The firm represented a company called

Redcats Group, which owns a number of plus-size apparel brands, including the Roaman's and Woman Within mail-order catalogs, the OneStopPlus shopping Web site, and the chain of retail stores called Avenue.

Ginger mentioned that Redcats had only recently purchased the Avenue chain. Until then, Redcats had been primarily known for their mail-order catalogs—catalogs I'd been receiving in my mailbox for years. Catalogs that came with unnecessary, forest-destroying frequency, often featuring identical clothes from one printing to the next, shifted around inside its pages to look new, with the occasional truly new item or two thrown in. They manufactured and sold clothes made from cheap artificial fabrics that adhered to your body with the slightest bead of sweat and suffocated your pores. Sometimes they made a half-hearted effort to adapt something from the runways of Paris to fat ladies across America, forgoing quality details that made all the difference, like linings or real metal buttons. Standing cheek-to-jowl with these designer-mocking pieces were the old fat lady standbys. Tent dresses, caftans, polyester elastic-waist pants with matching shapeless vests. I'd often shopped from these catalogs, out of financial necessity, always choosing carefully so as not to look too ridiculous. I stuck with the basics. Dark things whose poor quality and design might be harder to spot in black.

As a blogger, I often hear from public relations firms who target special-interest blogs, hoping for coverage of their clients' products and services. Ginger and I communicated initially when I did a write-up on wide-width footwear for women with chubby feet and calves. She sent me samples of rain boots from OneStopPlus—which turned out to be too narrow in the calf, incidentally. We'd shared a good rapport the few times we chatted on the phone, so I felt comfortable enough to throw an idea at her. I imagined having a relationship with Redcats might open a channel for showcasing my writing — albeit an unconventional channel, but a potentially far-reaching one. Besides, I liked the unconventional. And who knew? If a literary agent was exposed to my writing through some plus-size fashion-related project, maybe one thing would lead to another, and I'd achieve my dream of becoming a published author. I don't like letting opportunities die in my arms. I wasn't afraid to hear "no." Life goes on after "no." I took a leap.

"Hey Ginger, let me ask you a question. How come Avenue doesn't exploit viral video? It seems to me they could really win over their target customer with some well-executed branded video. Something that's a soft sell. You know, not a blatant advertisement, but more...say, philosophical entertainment. Something plus-size women can really get behind. Something with emotional impact."

"Umm...I don't know," Ginger replied. "I've never seen them use any video. Which is weird. They probably should."

"I realize this is more of an advertising thing than a PR thing," I continued. "But what if you could get a great idea to Redcats? Like, broker the concept or something? If they decided to use it, wouldn't you guys at least get a fee? I don't know how this stuff works, but it couldn't possibly look *bad* for 5W."

The video in my mind was clear: something like an extended TV commercial, but with a powerfully affecting, positive "live well *now*" message and *covert* commercial impact for Avenue. Me (in Avenue apparel, of course), addressing the camera, speaking from one or more of my well-received essays about being a plus-size woman. When my speech was over, the screen would fade to black and simply read:

AVENUE

Sophisticated in its simplicity, but no nonsense and direct.

I argued that the plus-size community had really embraced the Internet, videos and all. Our online network was thriving, I said, and plus-size news items were enthusiastically shared between fat bloggers, and fat-positive Web sites and chat rooms.

"Plus-size women feel slighted by the media and the fashion industry," I told her. "So we tend to get excited about anything that addresses us positively and specifically. I know, because every time I write about empowering topics that address fat women, I get a tremendous reaction. If Avenue circulates a video like this, I think they'll be applauded — even *beloved* — by millions of plus-size women. Women will consider it a gift, and in return, they'll want to shop with Avenue."

"Kim," Ginger breathed excitedly, "do you think you can get everything you just said on paper? Or get it to me in an e-mail?"

"Well, sure."

"I'd like to present this to my boss. Her name is Kellie Brown. She's the vice president of the fashion division here at 5W. I think this is a great idea and I think it's worth taking the chance to run it by Avenue. But it's got to go through Kellie first."

"I'll write something up and send it over within the hour."

Kellie Brown was sufficiently intrigued by my idea and

my sample essays that she did ask to meet with me. So I, her client's target customer, dressed up in a gorgeous taupe herringbone suit with short sleeves and cropped cuffed pants, a fuchsia floral blouse with a herringbone-patterned sash, and brown suede strappy heels. I walked with confidence and grace into their Sixth Avenue high-rise office, feeling like a valuable cog in the big machinery of humanity, feeling beautiful. I waited patiently for a meeting that would never occur.

Instead, Ginger and another junior staff member, Bridget, emerged from behind a glass door, flashing stiff, terrified smiles. I stood and they approached like wary kittens. I felt like a five-foot-nine guillotine.

"Kim, it's so nice to finally meet you in person," Ginger said, extending a hand to shake. Her voice was genuine and sweet, her smile still frozen and her eyes big and sad. She introduced Bridget. "Kellie is so, so sorry, but she was unexpectedly pulled into a meeting *just now* and she won't be able to see you today." She shot a glance at Bridget, who promptly began studying the carpet. "I feel so bad, I know you came all the way in from Jersey today, right?"

"I did," I confirmed.

Ginger made a sorrowful sound. "Well, if it's all right with you, Bridget and I will meet with you today and...and we can take notes that maybe Kellie can look at later."

I followed them into an empty conference room and we sat clustered at one end of the table. Ginger reiterated for Bridget some of what I'd said on the phone.

"Plus-size women will want to pledge their loyalty to the brand, embrace the retailer's name as part of their identity, wear its label like a badge of personal power," I enthused. Bridget listened and nodded politely.

I initiated some chitchat about the plus-size industry in general. I said to them, "Hey, listen — maybe you could give your client a little feedback for me. It's high time they started using plus-size models in their catalogs."

Ginger looked knowingly at Bridget, and Bridget nodded.

"I can't tell you how many women I've talked to who resent the Roaman's and Woman Within catalogs for draping these clothes over size-four models," I continued, "then pinning the clothes to death to make them appear to fit. It looks completely ridiculous and it's an insult to the customer. The message they're sending us is, 'We think you're disgusting and we won't stoop to representing you in our catalogs — but your money's pretty enough.'"

"We actually mentioned that to them," said Ginger, "but they say it's too expensive to use plus-size models."

"Oh, that's *bull*," I replied. "Models don't get paid by the pound. Even if they added one or two plus-size models into the mix, it would go a long way toward earning the appreciation of their target customer. They wouldn't have to replace their whole collection of models overnight. And they've been printing those catalogs for years, and always using the same women. It's time they stepped up and started respecting their customer."

Ginger and Bridget nodded vigorously.

I leaned toward them and lowered my voice. "And let's face it — most of those clothes are just plain *ugly*."

They laughed and rolled their eyes in acknowledgment.

"Yeah, like those big A-line dresses," Bridget piped up. "My great-grandmother used to wear those things."

"Oh my god, right? And the sweatshirts with *teddy bears* on them," I added with spirited disgust.

Said Ginger, "The thing is, though, a lot of that stuff

still *sells*. They have fat old ladies out in South Dakota or wherever who actually buy that stuff. So they have to keep making it, you know?"

I understood. "You're right, you're right. It's just strange seeing it intermingled with all kinds of other clothes. It's like they don't even know who they are. They're trying to cover every possible base that will put dollars in their pockets."

A pair of muffled voices traveled past the closed door and Ginger glanced nervously over her shoulder. Bridget looked momentarily uncomfortable.

Ginger gave Bridget a long, searching look. "Um..." Ginger noised, apparently not finding what she needed in Bridget's face. She looked briefly back at me. "Kim, hang on just one second if you would. I just need to...check on something."

She slipped through a small crack between the door and the doorframe and closed it softly behind her. After a few moments she returned.

"I'm so sorry about that," she exhaled. "I'm afraid Bridget and I have another meeting starting in a few minutes and we're going to have to wrap this up."

At the time I had no inkling of how many people actually read my little blog, and I assumed it wasn't many. So I was surprised when my story got picked up almost immediately by Gawker, as well as a blog by *Self* magazine under the title "Are plus-size retailers ashamed of their own customer base?" Soon after, the story was on The Huffington Post. Plus-size runway model Sharon Quinn reposted my blog entry on her own blog, complete with contact information for Ronn Torossian, president and CEO of 5W; Eric

Faintreny, chairman and CEO of Redcats Group; and Kellie
Brown, with instructions to "get to writing and blogging
my sisters. . . . It's time for Unity in the Plus Community!!"

I started getting e-mails from friends, acquaintances,
and strangers; a mixture of the regretful and the be-
mused; forwarding links to article after article about 5W
and its leader Ronn Torossian. The articles quoted former
co-workers and employees, former clients and would-be
clients, revealing Mr. Torossian's reputation as . . . well, basically, a scumbag. It seemed entirely likely that his fashion
lieutenant would be just the sort of person to unceremoni-
ously diss me. As they say, the fish usually rots from the
head down.

Next came the clumsy attempt at damage control from
5W. Adam Handelsman made the first call.

"Hi Kim, my name is Adam Handelsman," he told my
voicemail. "I run 5W PR in New York. I saw your post
the other day and I really want to say, this was a *huge*
misunderstanding. I would *love* to meet with you, have
you come in, talk with me and Kellie, and even Ronn.
And um, again, I think this was a—a misunderstanding. I would *love* to speak with you. My phone number
is _____. And again, I look forward to talking with you
soon. Take care."

I didn't believe there had been any misunderstanding.
"Love" to meet with me, he said, just *loooooove*. He said
"love" like he was trying hard to squeeze out a particularly stubborn turd.

I didn't call back.

The next day came a follow-up voicemail. "Hi Kim, this
is Ronn Torossian. I own 5W Public Relations," he blus-
tered. "I'd very much like to speak to you. I can be reached
at _____. Ronn Torossian, the CEO of 5W. Very much ap-

preciate a call back to speak about the truth, or...reality. Thank you very much, bye-bye."

The truth *or* reality. Or lies, or excuses made in a panic. One of those. I guess he'd decide when I showed up.

Maybe it was a form of psychic flash, but something about his less-than-crisp verbal delivery made me picture a chipmunk-cheeked little boy with a droplet of spittle oozing from the corner of his mouth, his mother standing over his shoulder with her arms crossed, forcing him to make a telephone apology. "I'm—I'm sorry I ate all your paste." A kid with a funny walk and a lisp, berated daily by a father in a gray flannel suit for not being "enough of a man"; a kid with a black speck festering quietly on his heart, spreading ever-rapidly as hormones morphed him into someone who was going to do all the screwing-over before anyone had a chance to screw with him.

I didn't call him back either.

Thanks to a newly installed analytics tracker on my blog, I noticed from behind the scenes several visits from Redcats, indicating that they'd read my account of what happened in their name at 5W. Since then, people have asked me if Redcats ever reached out to apologize on behalf of their buffoonish PR agency.

No. Never. In fact, it even surprises me that people *expected* I'd get an apology. I certainly didn't anticipate one. Not from a company headed largely by men that cranks out cheap clothes that are most likely made in foreign factories by grossly exploited workers, a company that prints out enough paper catalogs to account for a *third* of my total paper recycling every week, that pays spindly limbed models to hawk ugly clothes to women who apparently don't deserve better.

I guess they laughed the whole thing off. I guess they felt the publicity wouldn't amount to much impact on sales. Not enough to warrant any kind of action. Not even an apology that I could reprint on my insignificant blog.

In some circles, fat women don't matter. Even in all our substantial flesh, we carry less weight than the flimsy, dingy paper bills we carry in our pockets. Even within circles that claim to exist to *serve* us.

The whole thing reminded me of something I'd heard once at *Grace* magazine. *Grace* was a glossy, mainstream fashion magazine dedicated to plus-size women. Its forerunner had been *Mode* magazine, which folded, and many of its key creative players went on to create *Grace*. I had a paid internship with *Grace,* in their advertising department, during the summer of their one-year anniversary. I wasn't a college kid, I was a grown woman, but I had a feeling I'd learn a lot from the experience. I talked my way into the job with a heartfelt letter to the publisher.

My immediate boss, the head of the advertising department, confided in me that "every advertiser we get is hard-won." He shook his head. "I tried to sell an ad to Shiseido, you know, the cosmetics company? They wouldn't advertise because they said they didn't want fat women being seen at the Shiseido counters in department stores."

When iVillage blogger Leslie Goldman reported my story about 5W and Redcats, a comment was left on the Web page by yet another body image blogger named Stephanie Quilao. She wrote, "The PR on this story alone will have Avenue giving Ms. Brown a lecture no doubt. Whether Avenue keeps 5W on board as their rep is another story, but as this story spreads and if Ms. Brown doesn't share her side or apologizes, my crystal ball sees Avenue dropping 5W or dwindling their activity to almost nil because her actions will detriment sales and that rude attitude goes way out of the relms [*sic*] of Avenues brand attributes...I hope. Very soon, we'll see more of what both parties are made of."

More than two years later, it appears Redcats is still working with 5W, because I still get press releases for the OneStopPlus brand through them. And according to the 5W Web site, Kellie Brown retains her position as a vice president.

VIDEO STAR

"Have you met Kim Brittingham? She's our new video star."

"It's a pleasure." I extended my hand and let out a little giggle. I couldn't help it. Every time Diana used the phrase "video star," I thought about that song by The Buggles, "Video Killed the Radio Star"—the first video to ever appear on MTV.

Besides, the idea of being a video "star" was cracking me up. I thought you had to be on TV or in the movies to be considered a *star*—not just some blogger-turned-viral video host. And in spite of Rosie O'Donnell, Queen Latifah, Kirstie Alley, and Gabourey Sidibe, didn't you still basically have to be thin to be a star? Sure, I wished things could be different, and hoped eventually they would be. But in the current reality, fat girls didn't get the spotlight. Fat girls at best got to be supporting players, the token fat friend of the svelte star. Might things actually be changing for the better? Was the entertainment industry ready to fairly represent the population to which it was playing?

Every few feet or so, we encountered someone else to whom Diana Gaffney introduced me as NBC Universal's new video star. She guided me through a maze of cubicles on a floor above New York City's Chelsea Market. Plasma screens on the walls were either tuned to the Oxygen cable network (part of the NBC entertainment conglomerate) or played a looping video meant for potential advertisers. On screen, a multiracial gaggle of young women twirled in place with glossy shopping bags on their arms, or shifted their weight from one hip to the other in a sort of antsy postspending dance, as a narrator outlined Oxygen's viewer demographics.

Finally we reached a cluster of work stations where the women behind the iVillage Web site—another arm of NBC Universal—were tapping away on their computer keyboards. I was introduced to several gracious, glossy-haired young ladies whose e-mail addresses I'd come to know by heart, but whose faces I'd never seen.

"We're so excited to have you working with us," said Kelly Mitchell, a senior editor above Diana. "As you know, we're launching a brand new Web site within the next couple of months, and your voice is exactly what we're looking for. It's a *perfect* match."

This was encouraging. My antidiet stance was plainly counterculture, as were my views on radical self-acceptance where body image was concerned. I'd made no secret of them. My essays on the subjects were all over the Internet, including on iVillage. A guest blog post I'd written for them received a tremendously positive reader response, and it prompted them to invite me to blog for them regularly. About a month later, they amended the offer.

"We'd like to make you the star of your own video series. You'd create and appear in the episodes, and write a corresponding blog for each one. You know, something summarizing what you took away from the video."

I loved the idea. Here was an opportunity to speak to

women and girls on a grand scale about wellness topics, *without* pushing weight loss as a primary goal. America needed something like this. We live in a weight-obsessed society where the numbers of people with eating disorders, as well as the number of "overweight" and "obese" people, are growing. It's a culture in which the phrase *lose weight* causes a Pavlovian response in almost anyone born with a vagina. It captivates instantly. The promise of weight loss is linked to every possible product as a selling point. If advertisers could convince you that *curtains* would help you lose weight, they'd try it.

Not only did NBC Universal think my avant-garde notions were "perfect" for their forthcoming Web site, but they were willing to let a fat girl spread those ideas from in *front* of the camera. It seemed too good to be true.

Together we came up with a concept for the series. In each episode, I would address a habit or behavior I wanted to change—always outside the context of weight loss. I would seek guidance or advice from experts by conducting interviews, even putting myself in active (and potentially hilarious) learning situations, like taking a lesson in hip-hop dancing on camera. We decided to start with an episode about my addiction to chocolate, from the perspective of wanting to learn more about the nutritional value of chocolate, and showing that chocolate can be enjoyed, healthfully, every single day.

I was still wondering about the name of this promising new Web site, but up 'til then, it had been top secret. "Still won't tell me the name of this thing?" I asked Kelly.

"Oh yes, now we can!" she said excitedly. "Welcome to 'NeverSayDiet'!"

*   *   *

"*I know it* seems weird, but the more hyper and over-the-top you act, the better it comes across on video. Trust me."

We were filming the pilot episode of my video series, *Big Life*. The director, the assistant director, and the NeverSayDiet editors told me not to worry about scripting anything, that everything would come off better if I acted spontaneously.

I wasn't thrilled with that approach. At the very least, I thought I should have some bullet points in mind or improvise from within a basic framework of information. After all, they were my points of view that we were supposed to be getting across, and I wanted to make sure they were clearly conveyed. Still, I was discouraged from preparing. Instead, I found myself standing outside the Jacques Torres chocolate store in SoHo making a complete ass of myself.

I looked skeptically at my director, Nick, who was holding a sophisticated camera against his eye socket. "Wait, you want me to jump up and down in place like an idiot?" *Like those women in the Oxygen ad sales video?* I was thinking.

"I promise you won't look like an idiot," he said. "The more energy, the better. Try to look like you're really excited to be going in and meeting Jacques Torres, the famous chocolatier, in person. Clap your hands while you're jumping."

Sometimes when I hear a tidbit of good news, I do jump up and down in place, and clap my hands together rapidly, like a little girl—*goody goody*! But not with the brand of spastic pep Nick was encouraging. It just wasn't me. It felt completely and utterly fake.

Still, I gave it my best. This was my first video for these people, and I was trying to be cooperative. I wanted to be "a pleasure to work with." I didn't feel I'd earned any insistent bitchdom or divatude. Besides, I thought maybe I *should* trust him. Maybe all this exaggerated leaping and gesturing *didn't* look quite so stupid on video. After all, Nick was the one with all the experience in this field, not I.

While in the midst of my best impersonation of Jim Carrey jonesing for some Jacques Torres chocolate, Nick made a new suggestion.

"Now I want you to run up to the store window, where all the trays of candy are stacked, and drop to your knees," Nick instructed. "Throw yourself at the feet of the chocolate. Gaze longingly at it, maybe pretend you're licking the glass or something."

I didn't realize it until it started breaking down, but my "cooperative" spirit was like a rigid shell holding me inside. It was containing all the loose, sloshy bits that make me a complete person, including my opinions, my instincts, my harshest emotions. All the things we keep in check when we're trying so hard to be civil, be "nice." The things for which women must always apologize. The things that mark us a "bitch" when we wear them unbuttoned.

I felt cracks spreading across my shell of agreeableness; a gray crazing like marble. Then a flake fell, then two. New muscles tensed while others relaxed. My smiling muscles went slack. My forehead dimpled.

"I'm sorry, but I won't do that," I said plainly. "I'll run up to the window and gesture to the chocolates, but that's all." The video star was suddenly being difficult. Unmanageable.

Insensitivity toward fat people is so second-nature in our culture that it never occurred to my director that telling me to run hell-for-leather toward the Jacques Torres chocolate shop and drop to my knees at its window (as though simultaneously praying and salivating to the God of Chocolate) might be insulting to a fat person.

No, I don't think he realized he was perpetuating ignorant stereotypes. He didn't seem like the kind of guy who tries to be nasty on purpose. But that goes to show just how ingrained and acceptable the nasty habit has become. If I was African American, would this otherwise congenial, urbane young man have asked me to tap-dance into the chocolate shop or commanded, "Look at the camera and say, 'Mm-mm, I'd sho' love me some fried chicken with dis here chocolate'"?

Inside I sat at a table with Jacques Torres and interviewed him. I'd been told not to prepare, so I was without any scripted questions. I didn't like it. Not one bit.

Here I was, on the spot with my interview subject who was a very busy man, trying to think up questions between takes. It was awkward and unnecessary. *So unprofessional,* I thought. *If I was in charge of this gig, I would never do it this way.* And yet my name was going on this series. I felt largely out of control of the product and it made me very uneasy.

Still, I came up with some pretty good interview questions on the fly. Then Nick and his assistant began shouting out suggestions from behind the camera.

"Kim!" Nick called, momentarily moving his eye away from the camera lens. "Make it funny. Say that you use chocolate as a substitute for sex."

I balked openly.

Because fat chicks can't possibly be sexual beings? Because in their beastly asexuality, they predictably turn to sweets?

Hell, no. I wasn't going to perpetuate that kind of negative stereotype about fat women. Not in *my* video series. I put my fat foot down and refused to comply. Instead, I created a different question linking sex and chocolate, one that didn't presume that all fat women are sublimating their sexual appetites with food.

I'd expected to be drunk with bliss at the end of that first day of shooting. I should've been exhausted in that deliciously spent way—a soft-eyed swath of human linen wrung clean of adrenaline. Instead, I went home, sat on the edge of the sofa cushion, and shed troubled tears. Rather than imbuing me with a satisfying sense of empowerment, the whole experience left me feeling weak. I consider myself a confident woman, but this first video shoot brought up uneasy feelings from as far back as junior high school. I let myself be treated like a circus dog, performing with anguished obedience and hammy falsity because I was so eager to please. I wanted to be applauded for a job well done. I was disappointed in the NBC Universal people, and I was disappointed in me.

I went over the day in my head, again and again, trying to shake out and clarify to myself all the sources of my unease and anger. I groped for a way to make the rest of this project feel better.

Our second and final day of shooting took place about a week later. This time I was to interview a nutritionist about chocolate and shoot some street scenes that would provide a backdrop for the show's opening credits.

This time, I'd drawn up a set of intelligent interview questions and printed them out on a cheat sheet that I folded into my jeans pocket. It also occurred to me that we hadn't shot any kind of introductory statement for the episode, laying out what I wanted to learn from the interviews and why. I'd done no talking to the camera whatsoever, nor recorded any voiceovers that communicated something to personalize the video. So far, any fat girl could've been the star of this mess.

I scripted something breezy and brief but with a definite point of view, and committed it to memory.

As I took a seat beside Sophie, the nutritionist, Nick

and his crew worked on adjusting the lighting and hooked us up to our microphones. Nick asked me if I might like to take this time to think of some questions for Sophie. I reached into my pocket and pulled out my notes. "Oh that's okay," I said. "I came prepared," waggling the paper loosely from one hand. The interview was smooth and efficient. I gave them more than enough usable material with very few retakes, and I felt good about it.

Back outdoors, Nick had me frolicking and blowing insincere kisses at the camera in ways that didn't feel entirely natural to me, but again I tried to be a good sport and channel the playful part of myself. We were about to wrap up when I pulled him back.

"Wait," I said. "I put together a little introduction. I think you should shoot me saying it."

"Introduction?" said Nick. "Well, I don't think that's necessary. I think we've got everything we need to cobble together a complete episode."

It seemed we had lots of goofy footage, but not much of my actual voice, no real heart or message. "Look, it'll only take a few minutes," I said. "If it doesn't work, you don't have to use it. But isn't it better to have *more* material to work with than *less*?"

The argument seemed to work on him. "All right," he shrugged. "Go ahead, stand in front of the camera and say your piece."

I did it, and I felt better knowing I'd taken some concrete action toward making it a more coherent and personalized video, even if I had no control over what happened during the editing process.

In the final product, they used my introduction after all. In fact, I can't imagine the video without it.

My final contribution to the pilot episode would be the

accompanying blog—a summary of what I took away from my experience interviewing Jacques Torres and the nutritionist. I tapped it out, withholding nothing. I wrote about my director's attempt to put words into my mouth, and horrible, prejudicial words at that. I wrote about feeling disrespected and dismissed, and how it had seemed so easy for them to do.

I also wrote about how charged chocolate had become for me over the years, in large part because diets painted it as a "bad" food. I wrote about the many years I spent feeling unnecessarily tormented by chocolate—something created to be pleasurable. Popular sentiment made me feel flawed for wanting it and weak in character for eventually giving in—as if indulging in food was an evil act, on par with drowning a newborn in the bath. My inner rebel, in an attempt to help alleviate my misery at being denied what it wanted, cranked up the wanting of sweets so that I craved them and fantasized about them more than someone who co-exists peacefully with foods of all kinds.

I wrote about how making the video made me feel uncharacteristically foolish, and how those awkward days with Nick and the crew drove me to overeat in a twisted expression of previously unexpressed feelings. "Now," I concluded my blog, "maybe I can stop."

After Diana received the blog by e-mail, she telephoned to say she was "sooo sorry. We never meant to make you feel like this. I know Nick said some insensitive things during the shoot. There were moments when I just cringed. But believe me when I say we think you're wonderful, and you did an amazing job."

They ran the video on NeverSayDiet—but without the blog.

While I awaited word on when we'd shoot video number two, I watched the early development of NeverSayDiet. New content was rolled out on a daily basis, and I grew more and more confounded.

Zoom Zoom! How to Get Fit and Lose Weight the Zumba Way

Do you want to be featured on NeverSayDiet?
Send your weight-loss success stories to _____.
In the meantime, get inspired and check out
other weight-loss success stories!

Shake off the Weight with the Help of a…Plate?

Dr. Nancy Snyderman helps you lose weight and
some weight-loss facts that may just surprise you.
And, give you a little motivation to get back on track.

Summer Reading: Quick Tips to Lose Weight in Time for the Rays

One Essential Weight-Watching Tool

What were they thinking when they suggested that I, of all people, would be a "perfect match" for this site?

I received e-mails from viewers of the video who congratulated me on a wonderful performance, "…but I can't say I like the Web site very much. What's someone like you doing on a site like that?"

Suddenly I felt mortified to even be *associated* with NeverSayDiet. In order to view my video, visitors had to wade through a calorie counter, weight loss articles, and a sign-up form to get daily weight loss tips via e-mail. NeverSayDiet, eh? Stay obsessed with losing weight, ladies, but whatever you do, *never* call it a *diet*!

Soon NeverSayDiet became the biggest pimp of *The Biggest Loser*—the decidedly extremist weight loss television show on NBC. Multiple times a day, NeverSayDiet posted

Facebook updates attempting to engage readers in discussion about *The Biggest Loser*. *Would you vote off Ron or Mike for* The Biggest Loser *finale? Are you excited about the live season finale of* The Biggest Loser *tomorrow? What did you think of last night's* Biggest Loser *finale?* There were regular interviews with former contestants and the show's celebrity trainer Jillian Michaels. *Are you as obsessed with her as we are?* Soon the amount of *Biggest Loser*–related content on the site was so excessive, I couldn't believe they hadn't just dumped the *NeverSayDiet* name and converted it into the official *Biggest Loser* Web site. It was absurd.

I'm still not sure what the radically different concept of the NeverSayDiet site was *supposed* to be. People diet to lose weight. Whether or not you use the d-word is beside the point. You're either obsessed with weight loss or you're not. And if you're obsessively *pushing* weight loss, you're in the business of manipulating minds for maximum profits — period. You're just another corporate interest working hard to convince women they're flawed so they'll spend money trying to do something about it. What you want is for a healthy chunk of that money to land in your pocket.

In the case of NBC, all that I'm-not-right-please-fix-me money is collected in staggering advertising fees, justified by the hefty viewership of shows like *The Biggest Loser,* and high visitation statistics on its Web sites like NeverSayDiet — which in turn prod people to tune in to *The Biggest Loser. We promise to help you lose weight* equals *dollars,* from the pockets of millions of brainwashed women — like me, and maybe like you, too.

Eventually NeverSayDiet got back around to talking with me about a subsequent video episode. This time, it was clear they wanted no input from me. They had an idea at the ready, one that had no connection to any of the ideas

I'd sketched out some months before. It had nothing to do with any of the behaviors I was looking to transform, although they tried clumsily to sell it to me as a way to address my admitted anxiety. It seemed their real goal was to use my second episode to showcase their new favorite "expert," a personal trainer who worked for the Crunch chain of gyms. They wanted to shoot me going through a series of gym exercises under his supervision.

Working out in a traditional gym atmosphere was something that didn't appeal to me in the least. Those machines bored me. If anything, I was interested in exploring alternative, unconventional forms of exercise, showing viewers that physical activity could be fun, adventurous, even exotic. I told Diana, Nick, and Kelly all of these things. Early on, I'd suggested building an episode around me taking a lesson in light-saber combat, *Star Wars* style. Initially they'd been enthusiastic. Now they brushed it off.

I don't suppose NBC Universal's advertisers—the breakfast cereals, the cleanses-in-a-box, the many variations of enchanted supplements that tout weight loss—would've been too happy with my candor on NeverSayDiet, iVillage, or any of NBCU's Internet properties. Letting me run my big fat contrary mouth would've been too big a risk.

But I'd like to respectfully remind the corporate media giants of the world that with the greatest risks often come history's greatest rewards.

NeverSayDiet put my video series permanently on hold. I went on to create a series of my own: *Kim Weighs In*. Communication is a passion for me, and writing a script and delivering it on camera was a form I hadn't explored before NeverSayDiet. I found I liked it. I had an instinct for it. I got a kick out of scouting locations, collaborating with clever friends behind the camera, and coming up with giggle-worthy ways to convey a point.

I continue to create episodes of *Kim Weighs In*. I've gained the support of plus-size clothing companies who provide wardrobe pieces for the shoots and post my episodes on their own blogs. I have such a blast making the series that I think I'd keep doing it even if nobody watched. But they do watch—and some even write to say hello. They say they're encouraged by seeing a woman "of size" so relaxed with her body on camera. By some estimates, there are 97 million women in the United States alone who wear a plus size—and they rarely see themselves represented positively in movies or on television. That's a lot of women for a single industry to insult and shame. I'd rather take the life-affirming route and not wait for permission. I'm going to step in front of the camera and be myself. Let the images circulate around the world. Show that a pair of heavy legs, a set of jutting hips, and a generous belly don't have to equal misery. Show that life can go on even after gaining weight. Demonstrate that choosing to emerge from our hovels and shred our shapeless caftans does not have to be our undoing. There are so many of us. If we insist on living, those who'd hide us away will have no choice but to let us live.

REACH THE BEACH

I stood and skittered on light feet across the blistering hot beach toward the cooler, damp sand at the water's edge. It soothed my soles. I strolled into the frothy white surf, and the ocean rolled forward to meet me. It curled around my calves, cold and refreshing, and I gasped with relief, followed quickly by a lusty shiver.

I advanced deeper into the churning soup, my legs disappearing into the bubbling blue-green-white, the sweat behind my knees swept clean by a trillion tiny sand grains. Waves crested and the sun's rays shot through their filmy peaks, creating fleeting turquoise windows where hundreds of tiny fish reflected the light like shards of mirrored glass.

As the ocean rolled back out again, I saw clear to the bottom, a tan talcum powder carpet of pretty parallel ridges etched by the tide. With my every step the sandy floor yielded and surrounded my foot in curative coolness. A ruffled strand of seaweed brushed my ankle like a cat.

As the floor sloped gently downward, the water touched my upper arms for the first time, and I took a sharp breath. The oppressive humidity was whisked from my flesh at the water's touch. The antidote was shockingly immediate, and I shuddered with a pleasure that seemed to originate far beneath the ocean floor to travel through my body and exit on my exhilarated breath. I lifted both feet and propelled my body forward through the salt water.

I was weightless. I was the water and the water was me. I arched my back like a porpoise and dove under a coming wave. I emerged laughing. Somehow, here, in the ocean, I existed in a state of high energy and complete tranquillity, all at the same time. I could feel the space inside my body turning a serene pale blue as I merged with my watery surroundings. There was no pain here. There was no discomfort. Just my body, and movement, and a giant, salty, undulating basin cradling me, rocking me under a cloudless sky.

When I returned to the beach, I was smiling. I walked with ease. Maybe I even sashayed. Droplets of cold water on my skin evaporated quickly under the streaming sun. The sun was thirsty. I felt it laying itself over me, dressing me, reclaiming me for its own again.

Maybe this is what they call being in perfect harmony with nature. At the very least, I can confidently call it bliss.

Some fat girls avoid going to the beach because they don't want to be seen. They don't want to expose themselves to harsh criticism, even when it's unspoken. I used to be one of those girls, too.

There were other people on the beach with me, and in the water. I was aware of them. I even talked with some of them. But the whole gorgeous, invigorating experience of a day at the beach was entirely *mine*. It had nothing to do with those other people, or what they were thinking or feeling in the same moment. Nor did the experience have anything to do with my cellulite, the thickness of my arms, the protrusion of my belly, or my double chin.

I walk the beach in a bathing suit because I want to immerse myself in the entire sensual environment. I want to feel the sand on my skin, stuck to my sunscreen in gritty, exfoliating little bits. I want to see the salt dried in little white rings on the tops of my thighs. I want the coolness of the water rushing between my legs, I want the heat of the sun freckling my shoulders. I want the vapors of coconut suntan lotion in my hair. I want a wedgie full of pebbles. I do.

And I'm not about to swaddle myself in towels, sulk under an umbrella, and limit my personal joy because of what might be going on in somebody else's private mind.

I spent years feeling self-conscious at the beach. I covered up in all manner of T-shirts, capri-length pants, and mesh ponchos. If I dared to take to the water, the march between my place on the sand and the ocean was excruciating. I imagined I felt every pair of eyes on the beach boring into the dimples on my ass, scrutinizing my hips-to-waist ratio, taking disapproving note of the lack of definition on my upper arms. I tugged uncomfortably at my bathing suit, I sucked in my gut. I walked stiffly toward the surf, as though tensing my body might hold all the fat in closer to me, and jiggle less.

I made a dash for it—as much as one can "dash" with a body carried as rigidly as a mannequin. Ready or not, I plunged into the ocean without appreciation for it. It wasn't a pleasurable surrender; it was a forced and painful jolt. I just wanted to get my body under water as quickly as possible before someone could see it and recognize its imperfections.

There were times in my past when I lived with a constant concern about the conclusions other people were coming to, and the judgments they were making about my appearance. In my preoccupation, I missed so much. Not just on the beach, but everywhere.

Today life seems way too short for that.

I hear from other fat women who wonder, aghast, where I find the courage to constantly put myself "out there" and make myself vulnerable to public ridicule. I heard it a lot after my *Fat Is Contagious* experiment. *You must have balls of steel,* one woman said. *I would never do anything that might invite verbal cruelty. I get enough of that keeping my head down. And I definitely wouldn't go on TV unless I lost 100 pounds first. How do you do it?*

When it came to *Fat Is Contagious,* I believed in the challenge I was presenting to my fellow commuters. I felt that anything that encouraged people to ruminate on their prejudices was definitely worth doing. I also knew that my little stunt might draw *negative* attention—tempting unkind people to abuse me before a captive audience. I was aware that I might even make people angry. I did it anyway.

And just as I barreled ahead with the experiment itself, knowing full well I was volunteering for torment, I also went on the *Today* show to talk about it, knowing there'd be a vicious response. It was inevitable.

The same day I appeared on *Today,* I got an in-box full of hate mail of the most ignorant variety. Blogs that reported on my *Fat Is Contagious* experiment kindled dozens of juvenile comments and crude jokes at my expense. No surprise. People feel mighty justified unleashing their deep-seated malevolence on a fat person—and usually, with nary an intelligent point to be found anywhere in the mix.

How do I do it? How can I stand it? How is it that I'm not reduced to a wailing, quivering puddle of adipose tissue between the bed and the wall, refusing to ever open my trap or venture into the light of day again?

For one thing, I'm used to it. When you're fat, the world is plentiful with mean girls. Mean boys. Even mean little old ladies in calico housedresses. Like the one in the supermarket whose cart was blocking my way, so when I reached out to move it two inches to the side, she wheeled around and snapped at me, "Don't you *dare* lay a hand on my cart! And you know what? You're *fat*!" Or the man in his car, his beer belly snug against the steering wheel, who was paused at a red light with his window open and called to me with the zeal of a sixth-grader, "Hey there, hippo hips!"

When I encounter people like these, it's clear that in the moment, they have only one goal: to make another human being *feel bad*. Their aim is to create dark things and launch them out into the universe. Despair, rejection, desolation, pain. And in that moment, they've decided the misery should be carried through me.

Not everyone is so directly malicious. Every day, somewhere, someone is making a private, disparaging remark about a fat person's body to their best buddy. Somewhere on a Fort Lauderdale beach, a frat boy is shielding his eyes from a fat woman in a bikini and groaning to his guffawing friends, "Ughhh, I did *not* need to see that...."

Frankly, I see this as a sign of tremendous weakness on the part of the commentator. Come on, how sensitive does one have to be, to be unable to tolerate seeing a fat person? All you jokesters out there feigning nausea at the sight of my thighs, are your sensibilities really *that delicate*? Are you really that easily offended by a human body that just happens to be larger than yours, and its flesh perhaps more slack and textured than your own?

Your distaste is less a reflection of my "ugliness" and more a reflection of your tissuelike mental constitution. In particular, every time I hear a *man* making a remark about the unsightliness of a fat person, I can't help picturing an anemic, birdlike Victorian woman in a novel, collapsing onto a velveteen couch with "the vapors."

Maybe it's time to man up, ladies.

Recently, I was in a store browsing housewares, when a polished, brooch-wearing senior citizen stopped in the middle of the aisle, several feet away from me (carving out a wide berth around me, as if to distance herself from my contagious fatness) and openly balked. Her mouth curled up into a dragonlike sneer and she hissed, "That's dissss-GUSSting." She rolled her eyes in a perfect vertical motion, evaluating me from the crown of my head to my shoes. A man, probably her husband, stood behind her, and she spoke to him without moving her gaze from me, and speaking as if I was not just fat, but deaf. "I can't believe these girls today. Somebody needs to put a padlock on her refrigerator. She shouldn't be out shopping, she should be jogging!"

"Why do I need a padlock on my refrigerator?" I asked her serenely, enjoying the fact that I was about to make her very uncomfortable. Funny, they never expect the fatty to have a voice. They always, always expect us to drop our heads in shame and slink out of the store, fighting tears.

She didn't answer. She acted as if I hadn't spoken.

"Why do I need a padlock on my refrigerator?" I repeated, more loudly this time.

Now she pretended to inspect some merchandise on a shelf, and uttered something under her breath to her husband. I approached her slowly and stopped within a foot of her.

"You were awfully bold about expressing your opinion a few seconds ago. Why so shy now?"

She finally looked into my face. Her expression was so twisted with hatred, raw hatred, I was almost taken aback. She looked at me as if I'd been caught sexually molesting a two-year-old.

"You pigs don't know when to quit, and it's disgusting!" she snarled. "Someone needs to teach you when enough is enough! You need to follow the same rules as everybody else, because the rest of us are sick of looking at you!"

She put down a ceramic soap dish with a thud and rushed away, her wordless companion shuffling obediently after her.

I remain fascinated by this, perhaps more fascinated than I am in any other aspect of the fat experience in America. More often than not, when fat people are casually criticized, demonized, or attacked, it's for their perceived gluttony—and that gluttony is cast as something unforgivable, repulsive, antisocial. It's a point of view so pervasive, it provides the foundation for most fat jokes, and even the majority of "serious" discussions about how to "fix" the "problem" of fatness. So universal is the opinion that fat people are gluttonous "pigs" that it makes me wonder about America's deep-seated guilt as a materialistic, consumerist nation.

Isn't it interesting that we rarely cast a fat heroine in our movies (because it isn't what the public "wants to see"), yet women everywhere cheer for the pencil-thin Carrie Bradshaw in the *Sex and the City* movies and television series, who spends upwards of $600 on a pair of shoes...and whose husband's loving wedding gift is the installation of an entire closet devoted *to* those shoes? What else could Carrie Bradshaw have done with her money if she'd not chosen to wrap so much of it around her feet? In some parts of the world, the value of one pair of Carrie's shoes could feed a family of ten for as many years. If that's not gluttony, what is? And do you think *Sex and the City* would have been as wildly successful if Carrie Bradshaw loved *cheeseburgers* instead of shoes?

We feel righteous shaming a fat person seen eating an ice cream sundae...just before we turn and climb aboard our earth-raping Hummers, to motor back to our homes with spare bedrooms, and linen closets filled with both winter and summer linens, and our closets full of clothes purchased months before, still unworn and bearing tags.

Yet somehow, fat people get dumped on for taking more than their share, for being dissssGUSSting for not knowing when "enough is enough." You're a "pig" when you take more food than your body minimally needs to function. You're adorable, worshipped, and emulated when you take more shoes than your feet require to traverse the earth safely.

Fascinating, isn't it?

Don't get me wrong—I'm as big a material girl as the next person. I grew up in this country, too. Anyone who knows me well knows I like my stuff. I like my Jane Austen action figure, my dancing Elmo doll, my vintage dishware with the platinum rim. I like my shelves of books, my grandmother's porcelain-topped kitchen table, my leather booties printed with Warhol soup cans. But I'm aware of my condition, and it's a condition I share with most of my countrymen and -women. I'm willing to take an honest look at it.

Fat people also, apparently, "need to follow the same rules as everybody else." This whip-cracking sounds to me like sour grapes. Some people do cave to the "get and stay skinny" advertising. They eat in ways that deprive them of foods they enjoy. They spend hours upon hours sweating and sculpting their bodies. They live within certain limits so they can look a certain way. And anyone who isn't willing to sign up for the same inane sacrifices is abused. It's how they work out their frustration for living under such constraints. It may even be how they work out their frustration for *needing* to look a certain way to begin with. Maybe deep down, they hate being dictated to as much as I do. The difference between us is that I'm willing to break the "rules," and they're too terrified to try it. It all boils down to fitting in.

Being the target of such venom would have hurt my feelings, once upon a time. It doesn't anymore, because I took a moment to ask myself, why would I even *want* to win the approval of anyone so shallow or unkind? If you're ignorant enough to look at me and determine that the size and shape of my body makes me deserving of your malice, then I don't need you to like me. In my world, you are the junk food of humanity. You are empty calories, adding nothing nutritive to my experience of life.

It's so simple, and yet it took me years to truly get it. I can remember my mother telling me as a kid, "If they say nasty things like that, then they're not the kind of girls you want for friends anyway." Sure, I understood it. But the lonely feeling of being constantly on the outside made the words difficult to digest. All I wanted was to feel like I belonged, whether the inner circle was nasty or not.

These days, I actually feel embarrassed for mean people. Their perception of the world around them is crude. They are far from their own hearts. They're unable to detect beauty in anything that hasn't been served to them on a platter by Victoria's Secret's ad agency. They're limited.

They live distanced from compassion and as a result their lives aren't as emotionally rich as they could be. Even more pitiable, perhaps these people *fear* depth of emotion.

Or, if they do manage to be compassionate people in most areas of their lives, yet declare open mean-season on the fatties, it reveals that they're in denial about their own insecurities. They have a need to feel superior over somebody else. I find this particularly cringe-worthy, because these people don't realize how transparent they are.

As a grown-up, I can finally shrug off the nasties by the thousands, knowing with confidence that a more enlightened, accepting person always comes along eventually.

So what changed inside me?

I live more often from the *inside out*. What matters is what I'm experiencing from inside *here,* from inside *me*. It's what I'm seeing as I look out through these windows that are my eyes, what I'm hearing and touching and smelling, *whatever* I'm sensing in any way that feeds my heart, mind, and soul.

I'm not about to curtail *my* joy. I'm going to luxuriate on that beach in all my fat, flabby glory; I'm going to swim and breathe and sigh and dive for sand dollars and tickle the bellies of fish.

ACKNOWLEDGMENTS

Becoming an author has been my dream since elementary school. While it took hard work and much practice to get here, I couldn't have done it without so many friends who believed in me and lifted me up.

Deepest gratitude to my agent, Holly Bemiss, for leading the charge. You are my Boadicea!

Special thanks to Hillary Carlip and Rachel Kramer Bussel. If my writing career was a pair of boobs, you two would be its push-up bra.

Much affection to my friend Heather Maidat, who was right all along.

I can never, ever thank you enough, Andy Maliszewski, Sam Maliszewski, Stephanie Evanovich, Leslie Goldman, Carol Hiller, Pamela Skjolsvik, Beth Mann, Cheryl Burke, Stephanie Schroeder, Lisa Haas, Carla Birnberg, Margo Donohue, Liz Nealon, Suzanne McGee, Lisa Peterson, Christa Bourg, Gerri DiBenedetto, Linda Arbus, Frances Gizzi, Sue Brooks, Gina DeSimone, Danny Corrado, Toni Colaninno, Ron Colaninno, Randi Abraham, Jim Klaiber, Dave Asaro, Heather Sia, Agata Glinska, Zsuzsa Schuster, Jessica Rodriguez, Andrew Parfomak, Fran Foreaker, Charlene Tipton Baker, Shoaleh

Teymour, Jon Trauger, Hanna Trauger, Lac Su, Jeffrey Seeds, Bob Podrasky, Paula Newcomer, Judith Carluccio, Maureen Nevin, Pat Florio, Gail Aanensen, Kathryn White, Diana Jarvis, Joel Newman, Robin Margolis, Robyn Guido, Adda Gogoris, Rachel Fershleiser, Neil Cotter, and Teresa Cortez.

I am immensely grateful to everyone who ever read one of my blogs or essays online and took the time to send an appreciative e-mail. Your kind words and encouragement were this dreamer's gasoline!

I am thankful for all the bloggers and media professionals who wrote or spoke about me and encouraged others to seek out my work.

My thanks to everyone at Random House/Crown who rallied behind my book and made me feel welcome and enthusiastically supported from the very first day: my patient editor, Julia Pastore; Kira Walton and Melanie DeNardo; publicist Justina Batchelor. Thanks, too, to Jessica Bright for a stellar book jacket.

And finally, and most important, my love to Lori Bonfitto, for incomparable, everyday genius and heart.

ABOUT THE AUTHOR

Kim Brittingham began publishing her personal essays about a decade ago on the Internet, on Web sites like Fresh Yarn and iVillage. In February of 2008, she was interviewed on the *Today* show and National Public Radio about a social experiment she conducted on New York City buses. She created a realistic-looking book jacket for a non-existent self-help book titled *Fat Is Contagious: How Sitting Next to a Fat Person Can Make You Fat* and carried it openly on public transportation. Then she wrote about the experience.

Read My Hips is Brittingham's first (real) book. She wrote it in forty-five-minute increments while working as a patent prosecution legal assistant in New York City, typing away during her lunch hour in the law firm's kitchen, on a secondhand laptop she bought on eBay.

Brittingham was born in Philadelphia in 1970 and currently divides her time between New York City and Ocean Grove, New Jersey. When she's not writing, she enjoys designing and sewing her own clothes, traveling, performing in theatrical productions, and writing and appearing in episodes of her online video series, *Kim Weighs In*.

Learn more at www.KimWrites.com.

Kim Brittingham can be contacted by e-mail at:
hello@kimwrites.com
...or by sweet old-fashioned snail mail at:
PO Box 113
Ocean Grove, NJ 07756-0113
USA